A Ministry By Grace

Images of Zion's 125-Year History

Compiled by the
125th Anniversary
Pictorial History Committee
of
Zion Evangelical Lutheran Church

Zion Evangelical Lutheran Church
153 Nott Terrace
Schenectady, NY 12308

Published to the glory of God and
in honor of the 125 years of service to the Lord
by
Zion Evangelical Lutheran Church
153 Nott Terrace
Schenectady, NY 12308

Edited by Kim L. Lorang
Book Design by Carole Maiuccoro-Koch

<u>125th Anniversary Pictorial History Committee</u>
Robert Mielke - Church Historian and Archivist
W. Roger Barnes - Congregational Liaison and Treasurer
Herbert Hanke - Photographer
Karen Huggins - Researcher, Writer
Steven Rapsard - Image Selection
Richard Thron - Image Selection

Copyright© 1996 by Zion Evangelical Lutheran Church

All rights reserved.

Library of Congress Card Catalog Number 96-061795
ISBN 0-9655607-0-8

Cover paper Finch Opaque, 65#Cover -Cream White
Text paper Finch Opaque, 70# text - Cream White
Manufactured by Finch, Pruyn & Co., Inc.
Supplied by Hudson Valley Paper Company

Table of Contents

Introduction
by Susan May Haswell, Chairman, 125th Anniversary Committee v

Foreword
by Dr. Oswald C.J. Hoffman vii

Acknowledgments viii

Dedication ix

Honorariums and Memorials x

Benefactors xiv

Daughter Congregations xvi

Sons and Daughters of Zion xviii

The Formative Years 1

The Schulze Era 3

The Busse Era 19

The Transition Years 41

The Albohm Era 43

The Wildgrube Era 79

Zion Evangelical Lutheran Church officially celebrates her 125th anniversary on March 17, 1997. This book has been published to commemorate this milestone in Zion's history.

The 125th Anniversary Steering Committee was formed to prepare the projects and events of our celebration. It is with the deepest gratitude and admiration that I recognize the members of that committee: Jean Wildgrube, Norma Finke, Kim Lorang, Roger Barnes, Bob Mielke, Steve Rapsard, Dick Thron, Christina Knee, Dave McMullan, Marge Albohm Palmer, and Pastor Wildgrube. I am also deeply grateful to the congregation, the Church Council, and former members for their abiding support and encouragement.

The Committee held its first meeting on March 22, 1994. At that time Pastor Wildgrube put out the "carrot" by showing us the pictorial history book published for his home congregation in New Orleans. We "bit" and Kim Lorang took on the responsibility of leadership in compiling and editing this publication.

Kim has done a beautiful job of acknowledging all the talents and efforts of the Pictorial History Committee and contributors in the section that follows. In putting this book together, she became the working partner of the graphic designer. Kim's knowledge of computer capabilities and photographic and print media production very capably met the challenge of this undertaking. Her personal sense of dedication and commitment saw this project through to completion.

Zion's history becomes our own personal history in the joys of baptism, confirmation and marriage, and of loved ones remembered. The struggles and difficult times are here, too.

Our history reveals that the energy and faithful activity of our founders are alive in us today as gifts from God. His faithfulness continues through all generations (Psalms 119:90).

In His Service,

Susan M. Haswell,
Chairman
125th Anniversary Steering Committee

Zion Lutheran Church in Schenectady is to be congratulated on 125 years of history, making a vital contribution to life in Schenectady and its environs.

The pastors of Zion Lutheran Church have all been stand-outs. Each in his own way gave vigor to the Lutheran and to the Christian community in Schenectady. During these 125 years, our pastors served this congregation in its mission for Christ, each one leaving his mark on both congregation and community.

The ministry of music in Zion Lutheran Church has often been a model of what church music can be, uplifting the level of both worship and taste throughout the area.

Zion's reach with the Gospel of the Lord Jesus Christ extends to the far corners of the globe.

Praise to God for this gift of His grace to Zion, strengthening and empowering the people who worship here to meet the opportunities of tomorrow as they have during the 125 years past, with faith and love that are in Christ Jesus.

Your friend and co-worker,

[signature: Oswald Hoffmann]

Oswald C.J. Hoffmann
Honorary Lutheran Hour Speaker
2185 Hampton Aveue
St. Louis, Missouri, 63139

Dr. Oswald C.J. Hoffmann has visited Schenectady and Zion on a nearly annual basis for over thirty-five years to preach during the Lenten season. He holds the degrees Bachelor of Divinity, Master of Arts, and the Doctor of Humane Letters. He has also been awarded an honorary Doctor of Divinity degree from Concordia Seminary, St. Louis, Missouri and an honorary Doctor of Laws degree from Valparaiso University, Valparaiso, Indiana. In addition to serving as the keynote speaker on the Lutheran Hour radio program for thirty-three years, he has provided service to United States military personnel in Alaska, South Vietnam, Korea, Thailand, and Okinawa. He has taught Greek and Latin at Concordia College, Bronxville, New York, and held an instructorship in Linguistics and Classical Languages at the University of Minnesota. Dr. Hoffmann served as assistant pastor at St. Matthew Church, New York City, and is the recipient of numerous religious and secular awards.

Acknowledgments

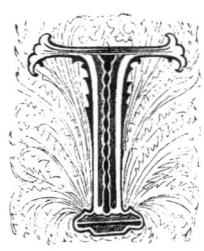

The undertaking of this project began nearly three years ago with the question "Can we at Zion produce a book for our upcoming 125th anniversary?" My reply was yes, but only with a considerable amount of work. With that caution in mind, the 125th Anniversary Pictorial History Committee was formed, and the labor of love begun.

The committee members who volunteered countless hours have been steadfast for the duration. Roger Barnes took the initiative as chief congregational liaison and treasurer. His attention to the details necessary for the advertising and promotion of the publication has been invaluable. Bob Mielke, Zion's archivist, not only provided the committee with a wealth of personal knowledge of the history of Zion, but also made available all of the historical documents and images in Zion's possession. His work for the committee became doubly demanding in March, 1996. Schenectady had experienced a sudden late-winter thaw coupled with torrential rains, and the church basement, where most of the material is stored, was flooded. Through Bob's dedicated efforts, many irreplaceable documents were salvaged and once more made available for incorporation into the publication. Herb Hanke's superb photographic skills supplemented the images in Zion's files, and Steve Rapsard and Dick Thron added their artistic talents to the selection process. The monumental task of compiling the text was ably handled by Karen Huggins. Her vast hours of research through old documents, records, and newsletters provide the framework upon which the book has been assembled.

There are also a number of individuals not on the committee whose contributions of information and skills have been invaluable. Ed and Bertha Schuler, Al and Helen Macholz, Pat Jones, Ella Weber, Connie Young, and Beth Bialous were instrumental in identifying old photographs. Frances Barnes provided substantial assistance in reviewing the text and Marge Albohm Palmer provided background information. Mrs. Trudy Lehner and Mrs. Carol LaRow, both of Van Antwerp Middle School, graciously provided translation and proof-reading services, respectively.

A very special note of appreciation is due our graphic artist, Carole Maiuccoro-Koch, of Caroligraphy. Her dedication and efforts (and all of our late nights at the computer) are beyond my ability to express my gratitude.

The final thank you is to all those individuals who have contributed images of their memories of Zion. May your memories live on in the hearts of all who enjoy this book.

Yours in Christ.

Kim L. Lorang,

Editor

Photo committee members are (left to right): Herb Hanke, Karen Huggins, Bob Mielke, Dick Thron, Kim Lorang, Steve Rapsard, missing from photo is Roger Barnes

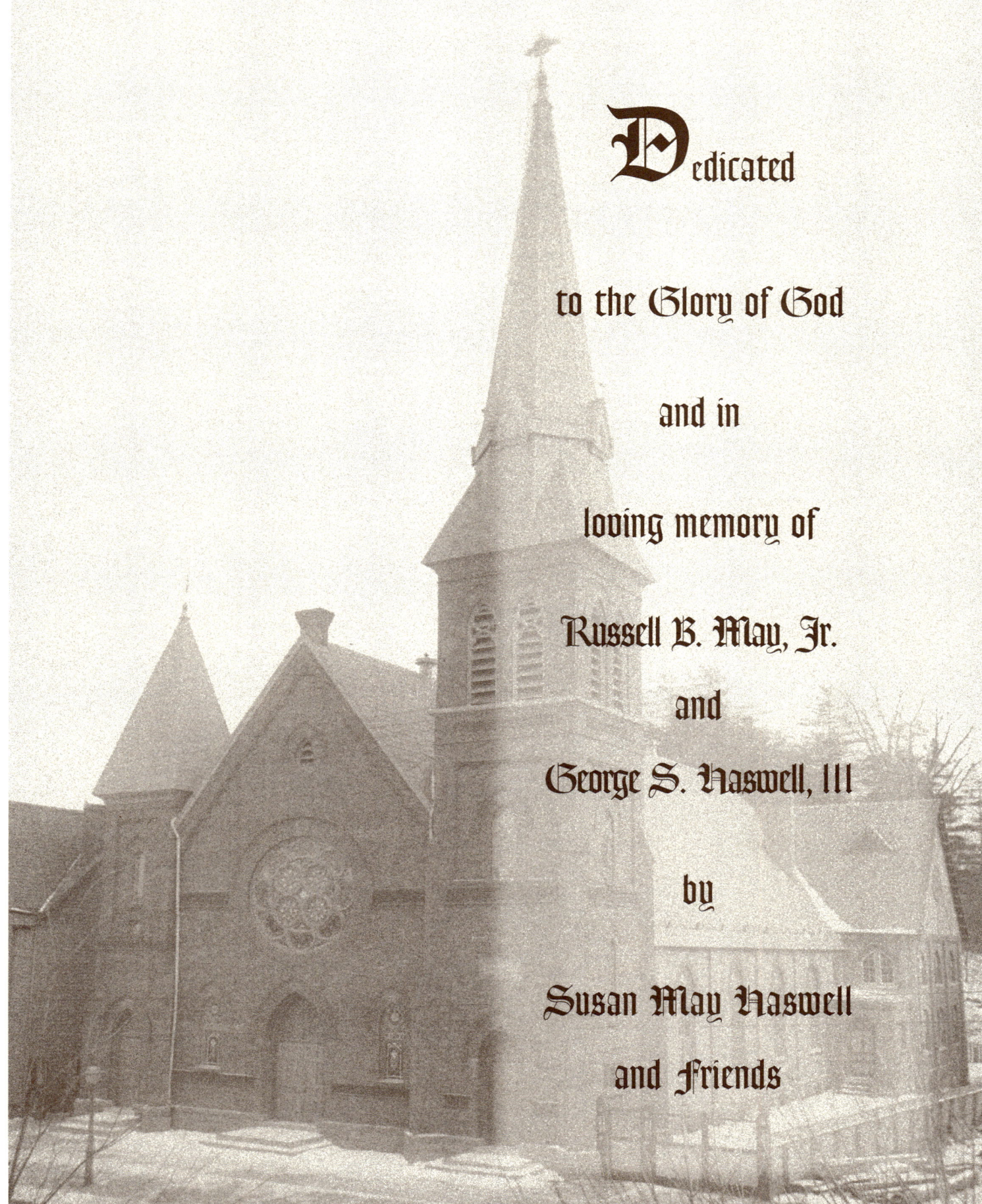

Dedicated

to the Glory of God

and in

loving memory of

Russell B. May, Jr.

and

George S. Haswell, III

by

Susan May Haswell

and Friends

Honorariums and Memorials

Contributions toward the publication of this book were given to the glory of God and
In Honor of

Emil Wilk for His Life's Work at Zion: Organist, Teacher and Church Secretary

In Gratitude for Loving Children and Grandchildren, by Frances and Newt Barnes

Scott Trexler, For His Faithful Christian Ministry of Music at Zion, by W. Roger Barnes

My Parents, Frances and Newt, for 50 Years of Love and Care, by W. Roger Barnes

Praise and Thanksgiving to God for His Countless Blessings, by Janet Bradshaw

Our Six Grandchildren and Mother Marie, by Bob and Bonnie Dietrick

Beatrice Finke Fischer and Her Late Husband, Charles, by Niece Dorothy Boos Wyman

Arthur and Avada Bodenstab for Their Lifelong Dedication to God and Zion

The 125th Anniversary Steering Committee for Their Gifts and Talents by Sue Haswell

My Parents, Jean and Alexander Huggins, by Karen Huggins

Rev. Gordon and Florence Johnston, by Their Children and Grandchildren

Pastor Carl Krueger for His Years of Faithful and Caring Ministry at Zion, by Friends

For 18 Years at Zion (1946 to 1964) In Loving Memory of Bob Albohm, by Joe Rynasiewicz

Ministry to Four Generations: Finkes, Sprengers, Sauers, by George and Martha Sauer

Honorariums

Honorariums and Memorials

Contributions toward the publication of this book were given to the glory of God and
In loving memory of

Edwin and Carrie Albers,
by Their Children

The Rev. Robert C. Albohm and Robert Carl Albohm Jr., by Marjorie Albohm Palmer

Rev. Robert C. Albohm, Robert C. Albohm Jr., by Marjorie J. Albohm

Dad, Poppy and Brother, Uncle Rob,
by Rudy, Judy, Jonathan and Liz Beyer

Son and Brother, Stephen, by Edwin and Beverly Andrews and Jennifer McGinn

Our Sons, Jeffrey and Adam,
by David, Linda, Eric and Dane Anker

Deceased Members of the Hugill and Barnes Families, by W. Roger Barnes

Parents, Ott and Julie Schmidt, Dave and Helen Barry, by Larry and Linda Barry

Wife and Mother, Marilyn Beltran,
by Adrian, Brent, Alyson, Darrin and Families

My Parents, Harro and Marie Wiebalck,
by Marianne Bergh

Wm. J. Blanchard, by Wife Leona, Edith Traxon, Ethel Egan and Wm. A. Blanchard

Clarence and Eliese Bodenstab, Wm. and Norine Smith, by Robert and Myrna Bodenstab and Family

Louis Glindmyer and William Bodenstab Families, by John and Carol

Husband and Parents, by Janet Bradshaw

My Dear Husband, Otto Brand,
by Dacy Brand

Our Sister, Marie Behrens and Brother, George Joos, by Edward Joos and Dacy Brand

Our Parents, Helene Bodenstab Joos and Harry Joos, by Edward Joos and Dacy Brand

Our Parents and Deceased Family Members, by Robert and Marilyn Brandt

Our Parents, Frederic and Caroline Brown, by Anna Brown and Helene Sprenger

Our Sisters, Clara Brown and Emma Lair, by Anna Brown and Helene Sprenger

Parents, Kristina and Paul Buno,
by Ann M. Buno

Ken and Ellen Batchelder, My Parents,
by Edith Calder

The Thomaes, My Grandparents, My Mom Helene, Aunts and Uncles,
by Barbara-Ann Carroll

My Husband, Edmund and Parents, Mr. and Mrs. Fred Glock, by Marion Dearstyne

My Husband, James DeNegris and My Parents, Fred and Amelia Ramlow,
by Marguerite DeNegris

My Parents, Carl F. and Louise A. Derwig, by Carl Schuler Derwig

My Maternal Grandparents, Jacob and Maria Schuler, by Carl Schuler Derwig

My Paternal Grandparents, Charles and Maria Derwig, by Carl Schuler Derwig

Douglas, Jason, Jim, Carl, Kathryn and Walter, by Bob and Bonnie Dietrick

Deceased Family Loved Ones,
by Margaret (Borcherding) Dimmock

Parents, Anna and John Hurta, Mat and Suzan Dobrucky,
by Bea and Milan Dobrucky

Honorariums and Memorials

Darthula and Joe Wilcox, My Parents,
by Karen Engelke

Edwin Paul Engelke Jr., Father and Husband,
by Matt and Karen Engelke

Our Grandparents, Myrtle and Robert Wellwood,
by Lynn, Diane, Sharon and Families

Beloved Uncle, Fritz Glindmyer, Love, Lynn, Ed,
Diane, Frank, Sharon and Brian

Beloved Father, Edwin Engelke for Your Inspiring
Love of Our Lord, Ed and Lynn

Henry C. and Louisa Finke, G. Albert and Marion
Finke, by Al and Norma Finke

Howard Froschauer, by Wife Gustava, Children,
Grandchildren and Great Grandchildren

Walter and Helen Lathrop,
by Edward and Mary Galusha

Parents, Armin and Emmy Schoenherr, Brother
Armin and Nephew, by Florence Grubey

Parents, Relatives and Loved Ones,
by Harriet and George Halsey

Rev. Francis Verwiebe, Son of Zion,
by Whose Hand I Was Baptized, by Marilyn Hansen

Husband, Hector Henness and Parents, Carl and
Rose Schneidewind, by Dorothy Henness

My Mother, Marie Hession
by Her Daughter, Marlene

The Aunties: Nellie, Bertha and Hazel Peper,
by Dave and Mary Hillhouse

Husband, Harold Hine,
by Shirley A. Hine

My Uncle and Aunt, Henry and Louise Sanders,
by Esther Horstmann

Horstmann Family, Frederick, Dorothea, Henry and
Walter, by Esther Horstmann

Henry Horstmyer, A Charter Member, Fondly
Remembered, by His Loving Descendants

My Parents, Lloyd P. and E. Isabelle Grobel,
by Jean Huggins

Our Parents and Grandparents, Henry and Louise
Kahre, by The Kahre Family

Henry and Sophie Meyer, Cornelius and Esther,
by The Kahre Family

Our Grandson, Samuel, Never to be Forgotten,
by Mr. and Mrs. Andrew King

Pastor Robert C. Albohm,
by The Ron King Family

John and Alice Knabner, John W. Knabner,
by The John W. Knabner Family

Husband and Father, John P. Leighton,
by Kay, David and John D.

Mother and Grandmother, Marie Mitchell,
by Kathy, Tim and Douglas

Our Grandfather, Kenneth H. Meyer,
by Natalee, Kennedee, Patrick and Kacey

Members of the McCrindle and Doring Families,
by Frieda and Jack McCrindle

Husband and Father, Harvey Mead,
by Wife Betty, Children Sharon, Doug and Paul

Henry and Louise Kahre,
by Iola and Robert Meyer

Henry and Sophie Meyer, Cornelius and Esther,
by Iola and Robert Meyer

Parents, Shepard and Betsy Allen, Louis and Elizabeth Peters, by Jean and Henry Peters

Kenneth and Dorilda Greenough, Henry, Frieda
and Ruth Priess, by Elmer and Jean Priess

Parents, Gustav and Josephine Priess,
by Son Michael, Donna and Grandchildren

Husband, Paul H. Ritter,
by Marion Ritter

John and Louise Heinz, William and
Bertha Bowers, by Jessie Bowers Roensch

Honorariums and Memorials

Erma Jean '80 and Dr. John '82 Rynasiewicz,
by Joseph and Dr. Robert Rynasiewicz

J. Edward and Martha Sprenger,
by Martha, Edward, Evelyn and Carole

Roger Fredrick Schonewald and Grandpa Bannon,
by The Schonewald Family

Ed and Stella Fensken, Albert and Nellie Schuler,
by Bertha and Ed Schuler

Husband, Father and Grandfather, Frederick J.
Schultz, by Agnes and Family

The Peper and Mueller Families,
by Florence Mueller Schumacher

Husbands, Dr. Paul G. Maier, Raymond L. Schwartz
Family, William F. Klingbeil,
by Carolyn K. Schwartz

Our Grandparents, Mr. and Mrs. Gustav Knop,
by Their Grandchildren

Alma and William Wolff,
by Lorraine and Charles Sherman and Family

John and Dorothy Strohmaier, Frances and Leland
Laupaugh, by Bob and Gail Strohmaier

Ewald Wagner,
by Irmgard Wagner

The Deceased Members of the Doring and Weber
Families, by Ella Weber

Frederick Wetzel, by Helene, Fred and Bettina,
Debbie and Jim, David and Kelly

Frederick Wetzel, by Jonathan, Brittney,
Robert, Matthew and Mackenzie

Husband and Father, Eric G. Winkler,
by Margaret and John

Parents, Rev. and Mrs. E. Wildgrube, Mr. and
Mrs. Louie, by Rev. and Mrs. Paul Wildgrube

May Wong, Louie Jeung, Anne and Bob Louie,
Clifford Hellmers, by Wildgrubes

Husband and Father, Donald Wolff,
by Joy, Kitty and Jon

Our Parents, Michael and Theresia Fix, Franz and
Elisabeth Wolny, by Fred and Resi

My Grandparents, Henry and Louise Finke,
by Granddaughter Dorothy Boos Wyman

Emma Finke Turk and Husband Paul,
by Niece Dorothy Boos Wyman

Clara M. Finke,
by Niece Dorothy Boos Wyman

G. Albert Finke and Wife Marion,
by Niece Dorothy Boos Wyman

Louise Finke Boos and Husband Louis,
by Niece Dorothy Boos Wyman

Lena (Magdalena) Finke Johnson and
Husband Arthur, by Niece Dorothy Boos Wyman

Martha Finke Sprenger and Husband Edward,
by Niece Dorothy Boos Wyman

Bryce W. Wyman,
by Wife Dorothy Boos Wyman

Our Parents,
by Glen and Constance Young

Benefactors

Archangels

W. Roger Barnes

Carl Schuler Derwig

Mr. and Mrs. George H. Halsey

Ken Horstmyer, Grandson of Henry Horstmyer

Robert J. Mielke

Thomas and Gloria Pettersen

Bertha and Ed Schuler

Morris and Yvonne Ziehm

Angels

Anonymous

Adrian M. Beltran

Robert and Myrna Bodenstab

Wendy Lynch, Cherie and Michael

Al and Norma Finke

Edward and Mary Galusha

Susan, Nancy and Families

Ruth S. Holtz

Karen Isabelle Huggins

Gordon and Florence Johnston

John and Mary Krueger

Marilyn L. Martin

Ethel Mielke

Bill and Anny Predko

Ingrid Rahavy

Mary Ann and Bill Schirmer

Richard and Betty Shopmyer and Family

Mrs. Edward E. Weber

Michelle, Michael and Robert by Gerd and Tracey Wolny

Benefactors

Saints

Anna Brown and Helene Sprenger

Bob and Sue Buck

Henry and Doris Bunkoff

Bruce and Kathy Heap
Scott and Glenn

Alan and Daria Iversen
Eric, Chelsea and Alyx

Betty and Steve Jordan

Frieda and Jack McCrindle

Mr. and Mrs. R. Schonewald and Family

Hildegarde Shopmyer

Gerald and Adele Smith

Una and Ed Spieth

Shepherds

William and Marlene Bond and Family

Margaret (Borcherding) Dimmock

Gustave and Janice Doepke

Paul and Marilyn Hansen
Peter and David Hansen

Jack and Ruth Harrison

Christina Knee

Leichman Family

Frank and Marion Mac Donald

Peg Mackey

Howard and Ellen Raust

The Richard Shopmyer Family

Kate and John Vrtiak
Kristine Vrtiak Gregory

Robert and Liga Wood

William, Linda, Laura and Michael Young

Daughter Congregations

TRINITY EVANGELICAL LUTHERAN CHURCH

On November 30, 1904, members of Zion formed a Mission Society for the purpose of establishing an English-speaking congregation. In December of that same year, construction of a chapel and parsonage was begun on Furman Street at the site of Zion's original cemetery. On April 9, 1905, the Society called Pastor G. Albert Schulze, son of Pastor E.C.L. Schulze, to be her first pastor. He was installed on the evening of May 28, 1905, the same day of the dedication of the new chapel. Trinity became an independent congregation in 1920 and joined the English District of the Lutheran Church-Missouri Synod. The gray granite modified Gothic church was constructed during the ministry of the Reverend Karl Schleede, who served from 1921 until his death in 1950. The education wing and fellowship hall were built during the tenure of Pastor Daniel Fiehler, who served Trinity from 1950 through 1960. Throughout her history, Trinity has been served by eight pastors. Trinity's current pastor is the Reverend Arthur R. Downing, who began his service in 1977.

Daughter Congregations

OUR REDEEMER EVANGELICAL LUTHERAN CHURCH

Our Redeemer Evangelical Lutheran Church was begun in 1924 as a mission of Zion. Formed to minister to English-speaking Lutherans in Scotia, a Sunday School was begun in the Scotia Movie Theater. The congregation was formally established in 1925. Pastor Bergdorf began regular services in the basement of the present structure in 1929. The church was completed in 1934, incorporated in 1942, and an additional education building added in 1959. Our Redeemer joined the Association of Evangelical Lutheran Churches in 1978 and participated in the merger that formed the Evangelical Lutheran Church of America in 1988. In 1995 Our Redeemer merged with Our Savior's Evangelical Lutheran Church of Carman/Rotterdam. Together they have conducted substantial renovations and building expansion over a six-month period in 1996, making the church more accessible and attractive for their growing church community.

IMMANUEL EVANGELICAL LUTHERAN CHURCH

On March 16, 1902, a special meeting was called at Zion to consider the founding of a church in the rapidly expanding Mt. Pleasant section of Schenectady. Five months after the purchase of a lot on Congress Street, a chapel was erected and dedicated to the glory of God. Under the direction of Pastor Louis Schulze, the congregation was organized and adopted the name Immanuel, that is "God with us". At that time, fifty-five members of Zion asked for permission to join Immanuel and organize as a separate congregation. In December of 1902, the Reverend George E. Schroeder was called as the first resident pastor. In 1948, the congregation authorized the relocation of Immanuel from Mt. Pleasant to Niskayuna. The church on Congress Street was sold, and a large home with an adjoining lot at 1850 Union Street was purchased. The new church was dedicated on November 27, 1949. Worship and Sunday School took place in the remodeled house, which also served as the parsonage. The current building was dedicated on January 23, 1959. Immanuel's current pastor, the Reverend Emil A. Witschy, was installed in March of 1987.

Sons and Daughters of Zion

Over the course of Zion's history, there have been twenty young men and women who chosen to serve the Lord by entering into the ministry. The fifteen men became pastors included Arthur Block, C. Henry Burmester, Theodore Buschman, George Derwig, Alfred Gerni, George Goepfert, Henry Heck, G. Albert Schulze, George Sommermeyer, Fred Thomae, F. William Wild, Jeffrey King, James Kerner, and Raymond Cummings. Four daughters of Zion entered the diaconate. They are Erna Heck, Jessie (Bowers) Roensch, Rita (Sadosky) Mangelsdorf, and Barbara (Looman) Town. In earlier years deaconesses made sick call, headed youth activities, did counseling, and worked with social welfare cases. Pastor Barbara Wegener is a ordained minister in the Evangelical Lutheran Church of America.

Rita (Sadosky) Mangelsdorf, on the occasion of her consecration as a Lutheran parish deaconess at Zion, 1955.

Deaconess Barbara (Looman) Town receiving her official call from Pastors Robert C. Albohm, Arnold Krentz, and Alfred Gerni at Zion on September 20, 1953.

Captain Barbara Wegener received her Bachelor of Arts degree from the Cornell School of Human Ecology. After working in the Graphic Arts field in Boston for four years, she attended SEMINEX, in St. Louis, Missouri, from 1979 to 1981. She returned to the business world briefly before completing her pastoral training at the Lutheran School of Theology in Chicago, Illinois. Following her graduation in 1989, she served her chaplaincy internship at the Lutheran Hospital in Chicago. She was ordained in September, 1990 and served Mt. Hope Lutheran Church (ELCA) in Shiloh, Ohio, where she remained for three years. She received her commission in the United States Army in the summer of 1993 and attended Chaplain training at Fort Monmouth, New Jersey. In September, 1994 she was assigned to the 72nd Signal Battalion in Karlsruhe, Germany. She remained with the battalion when it was relocated to Mannheim, and accompanied it to Croatia when it served as part of the Bosnian peacekeeping force. She has been in Germany for two years, and is currently stationed in Mannheim, Germany.

Sons and Daughters of Zion

The Reverend Jeff King is the son of Marlene and Ron King. A graduate of Concordia Seminary, he was ordained at Zion on June 3, 1984. In 1986, after serving for a short period in the Midwest, he accepted a call to serve Christ Lutheran Church in Southwick, Massachusetts. Under his leadership Christ Lutheran became the fastest growing Lutheran church in New England. His ministry has been featured in two books and he is a motivational speaker, addressing corporate, educational, and religious groups. He has been heard regularly across the country on the daily radio program "Day by Day", and is the Mission Executive for the New England District, Lutheran Church-Missouri Synod.

The Reverend James L. Kerner graduated from Linton High School in Schenectady and served three years in the United States Army. He was awarded the National Defense Service Medal, the Good Conduct Medal, and the Army Commendation Medal. He is a graduate of Concordia College, Bronxville, New York, and of Concordia Seminary, St. Louis, Missouri. He has served Good Shepherd Lutheran Church in Suffield, Connecticut since his ordination at Zion on June 19, 1983.

The Reverend F. William Wild was born in Germany in 1913 and came to the United States in 1931. Due to the scarcity of calls into the ministry, he entered the business world following his graduation from seminary in 1939. After a number of years he returned to the ministry to serve the following parishes: St. Luke in Putnam Valley, New York; Emmaus Lutheran Church in Ridgewood, Queens; and St. Matthew's Lutheran Church in New Britain, Connecticut. He has been serving the congregation of St. John's Lutheran Church in Yonkers, New York for the past twenty-nine years.

Pastor Raymond Cummings following his ordination at Zion, 1965. Photograph courtesy of Charles Ludke.

Minutes of the first meeting on March 17, 1872, written in German.

The original Jay Street Church used from the congregation's beginnings in 1872 until 1888.

The Formative Years

Zion Evangelical Lutheran Church is a community of dedicated men, women, and children striving to serve God and share in Christian fellowship. Throughout its 125 year history, Zion's members have shared many joys and as well as weathered sorrows. As a result of the Lord's blessings, the congregation has expanded and prospered since its establishment in Schenectady in the early 1870's.

Founded in March of 1872, Zion's first years were somewhat tentative as its founding members searched for an appropriate minister. From 1872 to 1880, there were four pastors called, each of whom stayed just a short time. In 1880, the first of Zion's four long term ministers arrived. Pastor E.C.L. Schulze was called to serve the congregation in January of 1880. His tenure lasted for nearly 40 years. He was followed by Pastor O.C. Busse, who came in 1919, and served Zion's congregation nearly 25 years. In 1943, Pastor Robert C. Albohm came to Zion to begin a ministry which was to span almost 30 years. Most recently the church has been fortunate to have Pastor Paul F.G. Wildgrube as its minister for the past 20 years.

The formal beginning of Zion Evangelical Lutheran Church was in March of 1872. On the 17th, members of the Schenectady German Methodist church met in the Congregational Church on Jay Street to hear a service by Pastor J.C. Severinghaus, a Lutheran minister from Oswego, New York. It is believed that the group, wishing to reestablish their Lutheran identity, felt it was time to form their own church, separate from the German Methodist Church. As the result, the decision to form the Evangelical Lutheran Zion Church of Schenectady was made. That name would not be changed until 1941.

A Ministry By Grace

The following week, on March 24th, the constitution of the church was signed by 61 men and 38 women. Pastor G.H. Brandau of Rochester, New York was called by the congregation on April 15 to be its first pastor. On May 4, the church was able to acquire the Congregational Church, where it had been holding its services, at a public auction for $3500. The following day, May 5, the members decided to affiliate with the General Synod of the Lutheran Church.

Pastor Brandau served Zion until February 1, 1875, when he resigned and was replaced by the Reverend M. Wolf of Altoona, Pennsylvania. Reverend Wolf was only able to serve the church until May 1876, due to ill health. Pastor J.F. Bayer served as interim pastor until October of that year, when Reverend Wolf formally resigned.

Mr. Emil Schneider accepted a call to succeed Reverend Wolf, but his tenure was short-lived. Charged with the misappropriation of proceeds from a "fair" sponsored by the church, he was removed from office on May 4, 1878 for misconduct. Candidate Albert Homrighaus succeeded Mr. Schneider on July 14, 1878. Following his request that one evening service each month be preached in English, the congregation deemed his leadership unacceptable, and he was dismissed on October 15, 1879.

Despite of the instability of leadership, the church membership grew rapidly. With nearly 450 members by 1875, the congregation had outgrown its structure on Jay Street. The decision was made to purchase the property at 153 Nott Terrace from Union College, where a two-story combination church and school would be later erected. This building now makes up the rear structure of the present church.

Zion Lutheran Church on Nott Terrace, as viewed from Eastern Avenue - circa 1895.

The Schulze Era 1880-1918

Pastor Ernst Carl Ludwig Schulze (1854-1918) - circa 1900.

Zion entered the year 1880 without a permanent minister. Albany Pastor W.A. Frey, who had shepherded the fledgling congregation on so many occasions, even served as interim pastor. It was he who recommended that Zion call the Reverend Ernst Carl Ludwig Schulze, minister of Immanuel Lutheran Church in New York City. Pastor Schulze accepted Zion's call and was installed on February 15, 1880.

Many of Zion's early members had emigrated from the Westphalia and Pomerania regions of Germany, and Pastor Schulze shared that heritage. Shortly after his birth on January 29, 1854, his parents journeyed with their infant son from Westphalia to Vincennes, Indiana. During his childhood, the family lived in various locations in the developing Midwest farm region. Although the family did not have much money, a Lutheran church in Indiana provided financial support for young Ludwig's education at Concordia College in Ft. Wayne. From there, Pastor Schulze attended Concordia Seminary in St. Louis, where he graduated in 1878. Following his graduation, he was called to minister at the New York City church, where he remained for less than two years.

Pastor Schulze arrived in Schenectady with his bride of one year, Louise Langheinrich, and their infant son, G. Albert Schulze. Albert was later to become the minister of the Trinity Lutheran Church in Schenectady, one of the daughter congregations of Zion.

A Ministry By Grace

Within two months of coming to Zion, Pastor Schulze led the church in a major decision. The congregation withdrew from the General Synod of the Lutheran Church in April 1880. One year later, in March 1881, Zion joined the Missouri Synod, which was Pastor Schulze's synod.

From the beginning, Pastor Schulze was firmly convinced that the best ministry for the children of the congregation was through a Christian school. Within two weeks of his arrival at Zion, Pastor Schulze petitioned the church council to allow him to begin a parochial school. A weekly school, which met on Saturday mornings, was begun by the end of February, 1880. When it was shown to be a success, the school was expanded to a full-time day school. It opened on August 30, 1880, with an enrollment of thirty-six students. A full-time teaching staff was required within two years to relieve Pastor Schulze from the overwhelming work load. He would, however, temporarily return to his teaching duties when unexpected vacancies occurred. The school climaxed with an attendance of 185 pupils who were enrolled in classes spanning the first through the eighth-grade levels. It remained an integral part of Zion's ministry until its close in 1931 due to declining enrollment.

left:
Zion School Grade Book, 1903.
Below:
'Zion Lutheran Day School' on Jay Street - circa 1880.
Shown are Pastor Schulze, on left and teacher, Mr. Kirchhoff, on right. #4 from Mr. Kichhoff Minna Verwiebe, 10 yr. old, later Mrs. Wm. F. Drees, #6 is Huldah Verwiebe, 8 yr. old, later Mrs. Karl Lunow.
They had come over from Germany in 1880 and were called "green horns" by American kids. It was recorded that they begged older brother Ernest, who had come over earlier, to pay their tuition for parochial school.

Pastor E.C.L. Schulze   1880-1918

Left:
Teacher William Meyer and wife.

Below right:
Page from **Zion School grade book, 1903**.

Below left:
A student's first catechism.

Zion Lutheran Church School pupils - circa 1895;
Teacher: Miss Turk.
First Row (left to right):
1. Mortsfeld, 2. Barney Schultz, 9. Ed. Sudmeyer.
Second Row: 5. Ed. Burmester, 7. Henry Sudmeyer, 13. Ed. Post.
Third Row: 1. Millie Meyer, later Mrs. Horstkotte.

A Ministry By Grace

First Row: William Coons, William Platt, Gustave Kirk, Carl Platt, Otto Stern, Edward Weber, Carl Spilker, and Walter Ramlow. *Second Row:* Carl Droms, Carl Blumer, Gustave Klute, Carl Doering, Edward Dettbarn, Emil Jason, Albert Buetow, Oscar Nitchmann, and Oswald Plunz. *Third Row:* Helena Hartke, Helen Thomae, Martha Thuemell, Esther Horstmann, Esther Bauer, Elizabeth Knop, Anna Siepmann, Esther Koch, Amelia Thomae, Alma Siepmann, and Rose Thuemell. *Back Row:* Mary Lantz, Christina Heck, Anna Heck, Anna Lohaus, Auguste Dargan, Anna Weiss, Clara Brown, Martha Plemenic, Gertrude Finck, Alma Weiss, and Florence Wagner. Teacher (Lehrer) A. Ernst Franke stands to the side (Elsa Franke's father).

Zion Day School 1916, Grades V, VI, & VII.

Years later, Otto Stern wrote of his memories of the school to local historian Larry Hart. He published them in the September 27, 1988 "Tales of Old Dorp" column in the <u>Schenectady Gazette</u>. Children would walk or take the trolley car to school. Teacher Franke taught all subjects to each of his assigned grades: including English, history, arithmetic, German, reading, writing, and religion. There was no gymnasium nor athletic field; so, the children would create their own activities for the lunchtime recess. They would pitch election cards and buttons, play "Duck on a Rock", toss snowballs, or play football with a five-pound sugar bag filled with leaves. There was a small bakery next door to the school where the students would buy a cream puff that cost a nickel.

One of Stern's fondest memories was of the school picnic. On the final day before summer vacation, the students would march as a group from the school to Brandywine Park, located on Albany Street, next to the Freihofer building. They carried the American flag with them in this parade. At the picnic, there were games and contests with prizes. The students' mothers made the picnic lunch and many of the mothers attended.

German Lutheran School lower grades Oct. 6, 1916.
Front Row: 1. Henry Heck 2. Edward Doring 3. Albert Doring 4. George Droms 5. Albert Macholz 6. Theodor Buschmann 7. George Rus 8. Walter Heck 9. Ernest Droms 10. George Singenberger; *Middle Row:* 1. Ruth Knopp 2. Dorothea Unger 3. Hilda Knopp 4. Hilda Quellhorst 5. Ruth Buhrmaster 6. Elisabeth Frank 7. Hilda Mielke 8. Olga Thomae 9. Madeline Plemenik 10. Elsa Horstman; *Back Row:* 1. Edward Beyer 2. Walter Horstmann 3. Karl Zamjahn 4. Arthur Block 5. Otto Plemenik 6. Henry Horstmann 7. ? Funk 8. William Doring 9. Alfred Heck 10. Henry Horstman. Picture donated by Elisabeth Frank Feruson, May 1977.

Pastor E.C.L. Schulze 1880-1918

Left:
Pastor E.C.L. Schulze - circa - 1880.
Photo courtesy of Carl Derwig.

Below right:
Young people's outing, 1892.

Bottom:
Congregational photograph, 1913.
Photo courtesy of Carl Derwig.

A Ministry By Grace

uring Pastor Schulze's ministry, many church organizations were active. The Ladies' Aid Society, which had begun when Zion was founded, continued to thrive. Pastor Schulze organized the Zion Young People's Society in 1881, which provided social events for its participants and gave them the opportunity to do fundraising for Lutheran institutions. The group later became a part of the Walther League in 1913.

The Zionsgesellschaft was a group organized in 1883 to aid Zion's members who might be ill or have a death in the family. The Zion Sewing Circle was founded in 1893, with Pastor Schulze's wife as its president.

This page top:
Zion's Men's Choir - 1899;
Center: **Zion's Choir - 1899;**
Left: **Men's Club - New Year's Day 1913.**
Opposite page top:
Church's Choir - 1905;.
Center: **Young Peoples's Harvest Party - 1911.**

Pastor E.C.L. Schulze   1880-1918

1912 Confirmation Class: Rudolf Poller, Karl Grobel, W. Arthur Verwiebe, Karl Verwiebe, Paul Mohlmann, Charles F. Fischer, Friedrich Lachtrup, Louis Forst, Anna Stone, Leona Stone, Karoline Drees, Christine Plunz, Emilie Dubberle, Helene Thummel, Wilhelmine Sauter, Jessie Ruter, Charlotte Neuendorf, Laura Mordsfeld, Gertrude Sengenberger, Elsa Blumer, E. Irene Degen, Esther Lunow. From Immanuel - Georg Pross, Herbert Heider, Friedrich Symoveldt, Elsa Peper, Ella Stein. From Trinity - there were five (names not listed).

A Ministry By Grace

1902 Confirmation Class:
Heinrich Maier, Heinrich Glindmeyer, Karl Kirschberger, Friedrich Kapmeyer, G. Albert Tiemann, Emil Weiss, K. Heinrich Hammer, Karl Mohlmann, Walter Derwig, Theodor Brandt, Wilhelm Post, Johann Koch, David Schultz, Karl Ossenfort, Elisabeth Sauter, Jessie Lange, Klara Wagner, Fraunska Holzhauer, Luise Pross, Anna Scheurer, Elisabeth Kusserow, Minna Butow, Emma Finke, Meta Meyer, Nettie Brandt, Lucie Springer, Frieda Freytag, Katharine Kadel

1908 Confirmation Class:
Fritz Hapke, Georg Koch, Otto Behnke, Louis Verwiebe, Friederich Freytag, Richard Gross, Johannes Schairer, Walter Mielke, Walter Wagner, Karl Linnow, Arthur Weiss, E.F. Wilhelm Bodenstab, Anna Spilker, Albert Unger, Rufus Maier, Walter Aldinger, Pauline Samulowtich, Karoline Kruger, Luise Blumer, Klara Siepman, Bertha Heinz, Helene Buschmann, Edgar Hammer, Klara Nitzschmann, Lohman, Julie Matthews, Emilie Weber, Ella Vogtling, Karoline Sauter, Susanna Heinz

1909 Confirmation Class:
Walter Dettbarn, Louis Pomplin, Karl Lantz, Walter Pluiz, Friedrich Holzhauer, Arthur Post, E.B. Anna Scheske, Magdalene Finke, Margarite Ackerle, Henrietta Karm, Laura Ruter, Maria Blase, Elisabeth Kadel, Maria Sauder, Jessie Brandt, Emma Maier, Lydia Kergel, Anna Schairer, Olga Degen, Johanna Freytag, Wanda Kryda, I. Charlotte Macholz. Confirmed in English in June- Charles Kircher, Fred Klauminger, Mathilda Lindemann, Esther Holzhauer

Pastor E.C.L. Schulze   1880-1918

1915 Confirmation Class:
Albert Schuler, Walter Beck, Albert Katz, Otto Pahl, Wilhelm Manteuffel, Karl Vogtling, Wilhelm Zamjahn, Friedrich Block, Karl Stigberg, Walter Verwiebe, Albert Glindmeyer, Herbert Neuendorf, Emma Hoffmann, Katharine Lantz, Erna Neuendorf, Georgiana Klauminzer, Ottilie Behnke, Elsie Kettner, Adeline Kergel, Maria Luise Spilker, Helene Braun, Irene Glindmeyer, Johanna Thummel, Edna Buhrmaster, Bertha Jockel. Plus ten unnamed from Immanuel and 7 unnamed from Trinity.

1916 Confirmation Class:
Robert Nitschman, K. Eduard Pahl, Johannes Plunz, Eduard Sengenberger, Hermann Butow, Wilhelm Block, Gertrud Blumer, Lina Lohaus, Pauline Schwarz, Emma Lachtrup, Helene Stigberg, Mildred Buhrmaster.
Plus twelve unnamed from Immanuel and six unnamed from Trinity.

1917 Confirmation Class:
Louis Drees, Wilhelm Mielke, Alfred Thomae, Wilhelm Verwiebe, Wilhelm Coons, Klara Luise Braun, Auguste Dargan, Martha Plemenik, Charlotte Katz, Helene Beatrice Finke, Rosa Thummell, Anna Weiss, Alma Weiss, Alma Siepmann, Florence Wagner.
Plus eleven unnamed from Immanuel and six unnamed from Trinity.

In the early years of Pastor Schulze's tenure, Mr. Emil Schneider had returned to Schenectady from time to time. Although he had been dismissed from the church under suspicion of mishandling funds, he continued to maintain hope of regaining a ministry at Zion. He was eventually one of the group which founded the Deutsche Evangelische Friedens Kirche in 1891 on Franklin Street in Schenectady. Several of Zion's members gave up their Lutheran faith and joined this church along with other Germans in the city. This was personally troubling to Pastor Schulze, but Zion continued to expand.

In contrast, Zion actively participated in the establishment of several daughter congregations. The Immanuel Chapel was founded in 1902. In 1908, the group was unable to meet its financial obligations, Zion committed to shelter the assembly. The Chapel remained under Zion's auspices until 1918 when it was able to organize as a separate congregation called Immanuel Lutheran Church and relocated to Congress Street. Zion organized an English Mission Society in 1904, building a chapel and parsonage on the Furman Street site. In 1912, the Society became Zion's English branch. The members of Trinity petitioned to become a separate congregation and formally established Trinity Evangelical Lutheran Church in 1920.

Two daughter congrgations pictured above.
Upper Left:
Trinity Lutheran Church in 1947.
Upper Right:
Immanuel Lutheran Church.
Left: Sunday School Picnic for Zion at Brandywine Park 1. Frank Dettbarn 2. Mrs. Dettbarn 4. Willehemina Fecher 5. Paster Schulze. 6. Mrs. Schulze. Emily Bauer Burmester is sitting in middle on grass. Picture donated by Bea Fischer.

Pastor E.C.L. Schulze 1880-1918

*The **stone quarry** on Van Vranken Avenue, owned by Frank Dettbarn, a founding member of Zion's congregation, in the year of 1887. This quarry lay between Van Vranken Road and the Mohawk River near the present location of Gridley's Truck Storage area. The stone from the quarry was drawn to Nott Terrace by wagon to form the new church's foundation.*

he church facilities occupied a great deal of Zion's time and financial resources. The congregation grew quickly, and larger facilities were soon needed. In early February 1887, the decision was made to purchase property at 153 Nott Terrace for the amount of $3,000. The parsonage was constructed by late summer of 1887. Following the sale of the Jay Street property for $3,600, the congregation resolved to erect a school on the new lot. Five months later, the two-story brick structure was completed at the cost of $5,345 and dedicated on March 18, 1888. The facility housed the school on the first floor while the upper floor was used as the church sanctuary. That building now forms the rear of the present structure.

***Zion's first construction**: the parsonage, to the left of the school.*

*The **first school and sanctuary of Zion**, dedicated in March, 1888.*

A Ministry By Grace

The city of Schenectady was experiencing unprecedented growth as a result of the new General Electric facility and the prosperous American Locomotive Company plant. Within four years, even this building became inadequate to accommodate the ever-growing congregation. It was decided on March 13, 1892, to erect a stately brick church. The new building was dedicated on January 21, 1893, in an all-day celebration with English and German services. Later that year, the $1,450 organ was dedicated.

Top: The church, as it appeared upon completion in late 1892. It was 54' wide with a steeple which was over 120' high. The structure cost $16,000, with the pulpit, windows, hymn boards, and Baptismal font donated by various church societies and in-dividual families. The building committee members included: W. Thomae, H. Sudmeyer, K. Lange, F. Mordsfeld, F. Tieman, G. Maier, K. Mohlmann, and F.H. Dettbarn; *Bottom:* **Zion's original church bell,** now on display in Zion's Friendship Room; *Left:* Traveling **artist Jacob Gogolin,** shown with his completed altar painting of the Resurrection, commissioned for the 1908 redecoration of Zion.

In the later years of the Schulze era, additional improvements to the church were made. The twenty-fifth anniversary of Zion was celebrated in 1897 with the installation and dedication of a new 2,075 pound church bell. The following year the church was redecorated and electric lights were installed. A $3,400 addition to the school, including a schoolroom, church council room, kitchen, and gymnasium was built in 1909. The twenty-fifth anniversary of the church building was marked by a celebration in 1918 and a successful program to retire the $3,000 debt incurred during the early building activity. The church was now debt-free.

The interior of Zion Lutheran Church, prior to ...

... and following the 1908 redecorations.

riginally located on Furman Street, Zion Lutheran Congregational Cemetery was begun in 1884. It remained there for only nine years. In 1903 Trinity Evangelical Lutheran Church, one of Zion's daughter congregations was formed and subsequently given the Furman Street property for her building. A new site for the cemetery was needed. The decision was made to purchase property on Albany Street. Over 300 graves were moved. To this day, the Albany Street site remains the congregational cemetery.

Original tombstones currently in Albany Street location. <u>Clockwise from top left:</u> Georg Selke, born 1884-1898; Christine Schult, 1898, Anna Schult 1899, Frederick Schuldt 1842-1901; Jacob Huber, Mary Huber & and Gertude Wachter, a baby born June, 1897 and died September, 1897.

Meeting of the newly formed Atlantic District of the Missouri Synod - circa - 1910. The gentleman holding the books, front row center, is Dr. Francis Pieper, president of Concordia Seminary and of the Missouri Synod; two places to the right is Pastor Schulze.

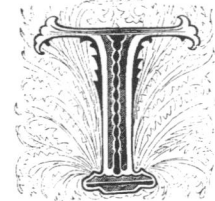

Throughout his years at Zion, Pastor Schulze experienced both joy and sadness within his personal family. His first wife died on their twelfth wedding anniversary in February 1891. Two years later, he married Sophie Sander of Ft. Wayne, Indiana. They subsequently adopted a daughter, Alma.

Pastor Schulze possessed seemingly boundless energy. In addition to ministering to the Zion congregation and founding Zion's church school, he wrote many treatises for the Synod on a variety of theological and Christian living topics. In 1906, he was elected President of the new Atlantic District of the Missouri Synod, a post which he held until his death. He was known for traveling to other congregations in the district for meetings and services. He also served as chairman of the Missouri Synod's College of Presidents. It was widely believed that Pastor Schulze's high level of enthusiasm and activities took a great toll on his health, and when the worldwide influenza epidemic hit the Schenectady community in 1918, Pastor Schulze no longer had the strength to fight the infection. He succumbed within just a few days of becoming ill and was counted among the thousands who died.

From left to right: ***Schulze tombstone*** *front view;* ***Zions Glocke****, the weekly newsletter of the Church; Schulze tombstone rear view.*

Zions Glocke

Erscheint im Dienst der evang.-luth. Zions-Kirche zu Schenectady, N. Y. in der Regel den 2. Sonntag jeden Monats. Bezahlung wird nicht gefordert, wer aber das gute Werk derselben unterstützen will, gibt dafür jährlich 50 Cts. oder wieviel er will.

Jahrgang 22. November 1918. No. 11

Ev.-Luth. Zions-Kirche,
Nott Terrace.

Gottesdienst: Sonntagmorgen um ½11, Sonntagabend um ½8 Uhr. Englisch 2. und 4. Sonntagabend jeden Monats.
Sonntagschule: Nach dem Morgengottesdienst von 12—1 Uhr.
Wochenschule, zwei Klassen: Von Montag bis Freitag.
Gottesacker an der Albany Straße, Hale Straße gegenüber. Sekretär: A. Derwig, 18 Barrett Str.

Immanuels-Kirche, Congreß Str.
Pastor: C. Kreymann, 417 Congreß Str., am sichersten daheim zu finden am Freitagabend.
Gottesdienst: Jeden Sonntagmorgen 10 Uhr.
Sonntagschule: Immer nach dem Gottesdienst, um ½12 Uhr.
Samstagsschule: Vormittags um 9 Uhr, gehalten vom Pastor.

Trinity Ev. Luth. Chapel,
Furman Street.
R. Siebert, Pastor., 11 Furman St.
Services: Sunday morning at 10.30. Sunday evening at 7.30. Sunday school at noon.

† Pastor E. C. Louis Schulze. †
weiland Seelsorger unserer Gemeinde vom 15. Febr. 1880 bis 9. Okt. 1918.

Im Januar 1880 wurde unser treuverdienter Pastor Schulze weg berufen nach hier, von der Immanuels-Gemeinde an der 83. Straße zwischen 2. u. 3. Avenue, N. Y. City. Am 15. Februar wurde er im Morgengottesdienst hier eingeführt und am Abend hielt er seine Antrittspredigt; der Text war Matth. 10, 34: „Ich bin nicht gekommen Frieden zu senden, sondern das Schwert."

Er hat das Schwert des göttlichen Gesetzes in rechter Weise und zur rechten Zeit gehandhabt, aber auch stets den Frieden des süßen Evangeliums verkündigt von der Kanzel, bei Leichenreden und privat Seelsorge, das muß ihm Feind wie Freund nachrühmen. — Wir trauern über seinen plötzlichen Verlust, doch der Erzhirte und Bischof unserer Seelen, der die Wunde hat schlagen lassen, wird dieselbe wieder heilen und unsere Traurigkeit wieder in Freude verwandeln, wann seine Zeit es zu tun gekommen ist, bis dahin halten wir stille und lassen ihn walten. Getauft wurden von ihm 1888 Kinder, konfirmiert 696 Kinder, es kommunizierten bei ihm 15,469, getraut wurden 350 Paare, Leichenreden hielt er an 679 Särgen und sein Leib ist der 680te der nun am 12. Oktober auf unserm Friedhofe zu seiner letzten Ruhe in die Erde gebettet wurde. Er hat unsere Gemeindeschule gegründet, indem er ein und einhalbes Jahr selbst Schule hielt und, nachdem im Jahre 1882 die Gemeinde einen Lehrer berief, stets für die christliche Wochenschule gewirkt und geredet, noch besonders in unserer letzten regelmäßigen Gemeinde-Versammlung am 16. September. — Er war der Gründer unsers Frauenvereins und diente demselben die ganze Zeit als Sekretär und Schatzmeister.

Der konfirmierten Jugend ist er treulich nachgegangen, ist stets, wenn nicht verhindert, bei den Versammlungen unsers Jünglings- und Jungfrauenvereins zugegen gewesen und hat mit Rat und Anweisung denselben geleitet. Er war Gründer der unter uns bestehenden Zionsgesellschaft. — In den Gemeinde-Versammlungen war er Leiter und Berater und hatte die Gabe, die Finanzen zum Vorteil der Gemeinde zu leiten, so daß am letzten 31. Juli ein Schuldentilgungsfest gefeiert werden konnte.

Wir wollen es nicht versäumen, Gott für die Wohltaten, die durch ihn uns zugeflossen sind, zu danken; wir behalten seiner in stetigem freundlichen Angedenken. — Ihm ist nun wohl, er ruht von seiner Arbeit und seine Werke folgen ihm nach. —

A. C. F.

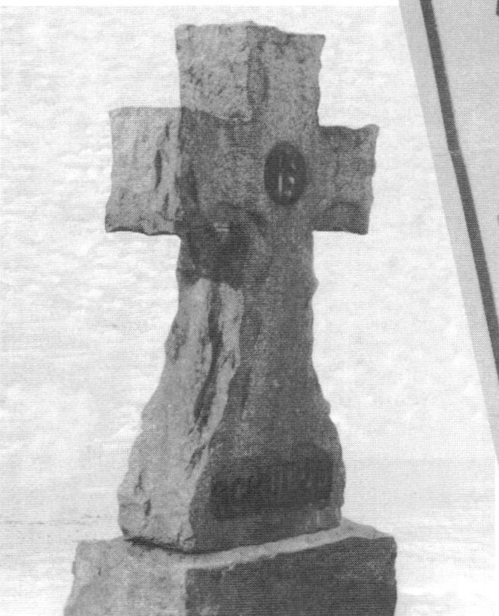

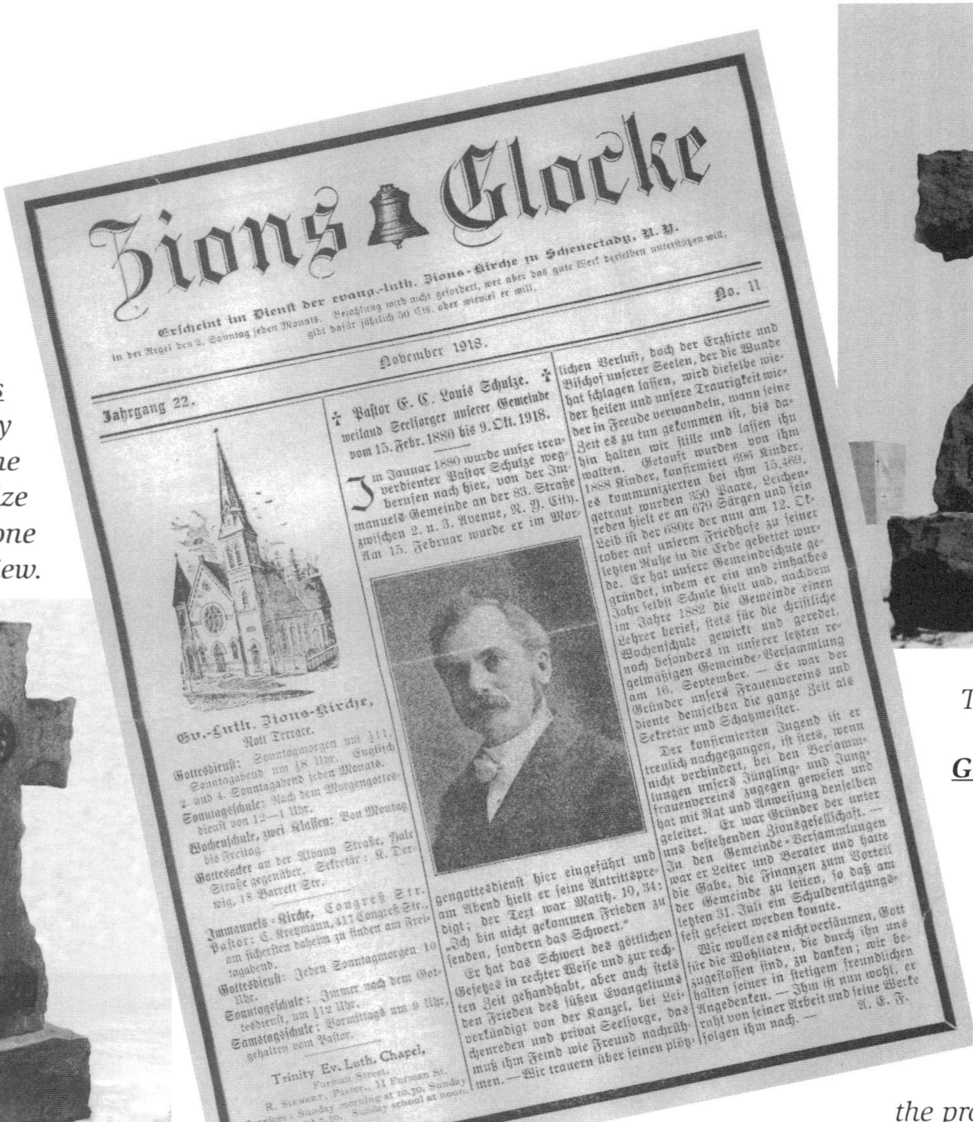

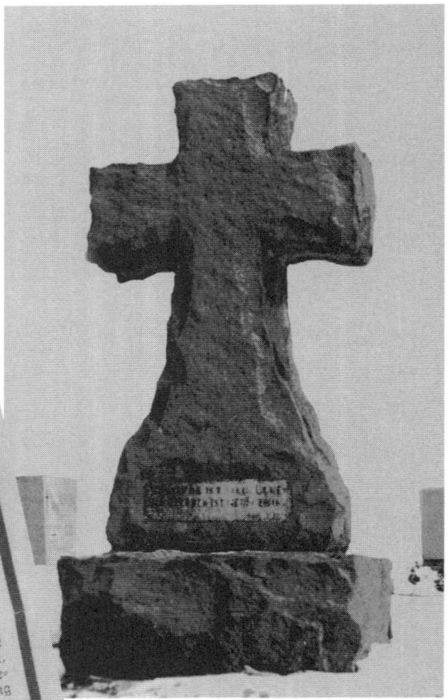

The ***November, 1918 issue of the Zions Glocke*** *announcing the death of Pastor E.C. Louis Schulze on October 9, 1918. He was interred in the Zion Cemetery on October 12. The memorial service was postponed for some time due to the prohibition of public funeral services in an effort to stem the spread of influenza.*

Pastor Otto Carl Busse (1889-1984) - circa 1919.

The Busse Era 1919-1945

he void left by the loss of Pastor Schulze would continue through the winter of 1918 until spring, 1919, when the Reverend Otto C. Busse accepted the call to serve Zion's congregation. The son of Frederick and Louise (nee Rodenbeck), he was reared in Fort Wayne and Decatur, Indiana. Like Pastor Schulze, Pastor Busse was a graduate of Concordia College in Fort Wayne and of Concordia Theological Seminary, located in St. Louis. He completed additional studies at the University of Texas.

Following his graduation in 1913, Pastor Busse was ordained in San Antonio, Texas, where he organized St. Paul's Lutheran Church. He served as pastor of St. John's Lutheran Church in Rochester, Indiana from 1916 to 1918, at which time he joined the United States Army and served as a chaplain at Camp Sherman, Ohio. Pastor Busse came to Zion upon being relieved from active duty, bringing with him his wife of five years, the former Helen Miller, and their young daughter Ruth. He was installed on April 27, 1919.

While the one and one-half year involvement of the United States in the fighting in World War I had a profound effect on many American families, Zion's congregation was relatively unscathed. Of the twenty-four members who served in the United States Navy, and one who served as a Red Cross nurse, all returned safely. This blessing was celebrated with a Service of Thanksgiving on September 21, 1919.

The year 1919 was also the year that Zion's size and influence were sufficient to command synod attention. That year, at the Synodical Conference held at Zion from May 14 through 20, Zion's contribution of more that $2,300.00 made it possible to establish the Endowment Fund of the Lutheran Layman's League for the support of disabled pastors, teachers, their wives and orphaned children.

The fiftieth anniversary of Zion was highlighted in 1922 with a week-long celebration, from May 21 to May 28. Sunday services in both German and English were conducted, as well as evening services throughout the week. Special contributions in honor of the anniversary were used to purchase new lighting fixtures and also provide for the refurbishing of the oil paintings which adorned the walls in the front of the sanctuary. To commemorate the event, the Jubilee Committee published *The History of Zion Evangelical Lutheran Church*, written in German and English.

*The **Ninth Convention of the Atlantic District** Held at Zion, May 14-20, 1919.*

Top: **Young People's Production, Circa 1920.** Photograph courtesy of Carl Derwig.
Middle: **"Order of Festival Services and Program for Zion's Fiftieth Anniversary"** pamphlet cover.
Bottom photographs: Details of the **lateral paintings** in the front of the sanctuary, 1922.

A Ministry By Grace

Throughout the 1920's Zion continually struggled with the language issue. Following the end of World War I there had been a substantial influx of immigrants from Germany. This, coupled with the establishment of Trinity as a separate English-speaking congregation, provided strong support for the continued use of German as the principal language of worship at Zion. Nevertheless, there was a growing sentiment for the provision for English services on Sunday mornings. As the result, in 1923 it was decided to adopt a schedule of Sunday morning and evening services which alternated the use of English and German. This schedule was put into effect in the fall of 1923.

In a congregational vote in 1927, the issue was again addressed. It was decided to further arrange the worship

Above and left: **Minutes of the same Congregational Meeting** *in English and German, September 12, 1938.*
Next page: *An early photograph of* **Our Redeemer Lutheran Church.**

schedule so that there would be complete parity over a two year span between the number of services conducted in English and those conducted in German. Finally, in 1929, it was established at a special congregational meeting that there would be both an English and a German service conducted every Sunday morning. The Diamond Anniversary Booklet noted that the church minutes recorded the presence of women at the special congregational meeting, for the first time in Zion's history.

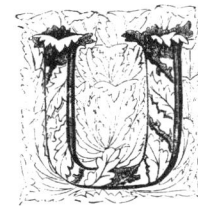
nder Pastor Busse's leadership, Zion continued her tradition of developing and supporting mission groups. Immanuel Lutheran Church had become self-supporting by the end of Pastor Schulze's tenure. In 1920, Trinity Evangelical Lutheran Church, Zion's former English Mission Society, formally became independent. Zion, however, was to later provide additional support in 1927 by holding a mortgage on Trinity's Furman Street chapel. This was done as a means of providing the finances needed by Trinity to build a new structure.

The Mission Society of Schenectady, with Zion's active support, established a Sunday School in Scotia in 1926. Two years later Zion advanced to the Sunday School the funds needed to build a small church. As the group continued to grow, a pastor was called and Our Redeemer Lutheran Church of Scotia was formed.

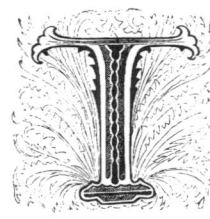The prosperity which blessed the nation in general, and Schenectady in particular, following the end of World War I did not positively affect Zion in all aspects. As the quality of education provided by public schools improved, the need for parochial schools lessened. By 1923, enrollment in Zion's full-time school had dropped from 185 students in 1880 to only forty-eight students. Schenectady's school system now included a junior-high school, and it was subsequently decided to eliminate the 7th and 8th grades from Zion's program. In 1931 Zion's congregation overwhelmingly passed a referendum to close the parochial school. Weekday religious instruction now took place under the state's release-time program. This program provided for the early release from public school instruction so that students could attend religious instruction. Zion continued to provide Saturday religious classes as well.

Zion's members were not spared hardship when the stock market collapsed on October 24, 1929, Black

*Excerpt of **January, 1931 minutes** reporting the referendum results approving the closing of the parochial school.*

Thursday, bringing the economic community of the nation to its knees. As the economy spiraled downward through the early 1930's, many lost their jobs. Those who were fortunate enough to remain employed were forced to take salary cutbacks which amounted to as much as half their pre-Depression income. In 1934, when the Depression had hit its deepest point, Pastor Busse, as well as the sexton and organist made "salary refunds" to the amount of fifty percent of their respective earnings. The Depression's grip on the nation gradually loosened under President Roosevelt's "New Deal" policies in the latter half of the of the 1930's. By January, 1937 Zion's members had realized sufficient financial recovery to reduce the church staff's "salary refunds" to twenty-five percent, and in September that same year the refunds were ended completely. Spiritually, however, the congregation had not fully recovered. The preoccupation of members with their personal economic and family affairs was evidenced by the lack of participation in church work. On four separate occasions in 1936, attendance of the congregational meetings was so sparse that a quorum could not be established, and the meetings were canceled.

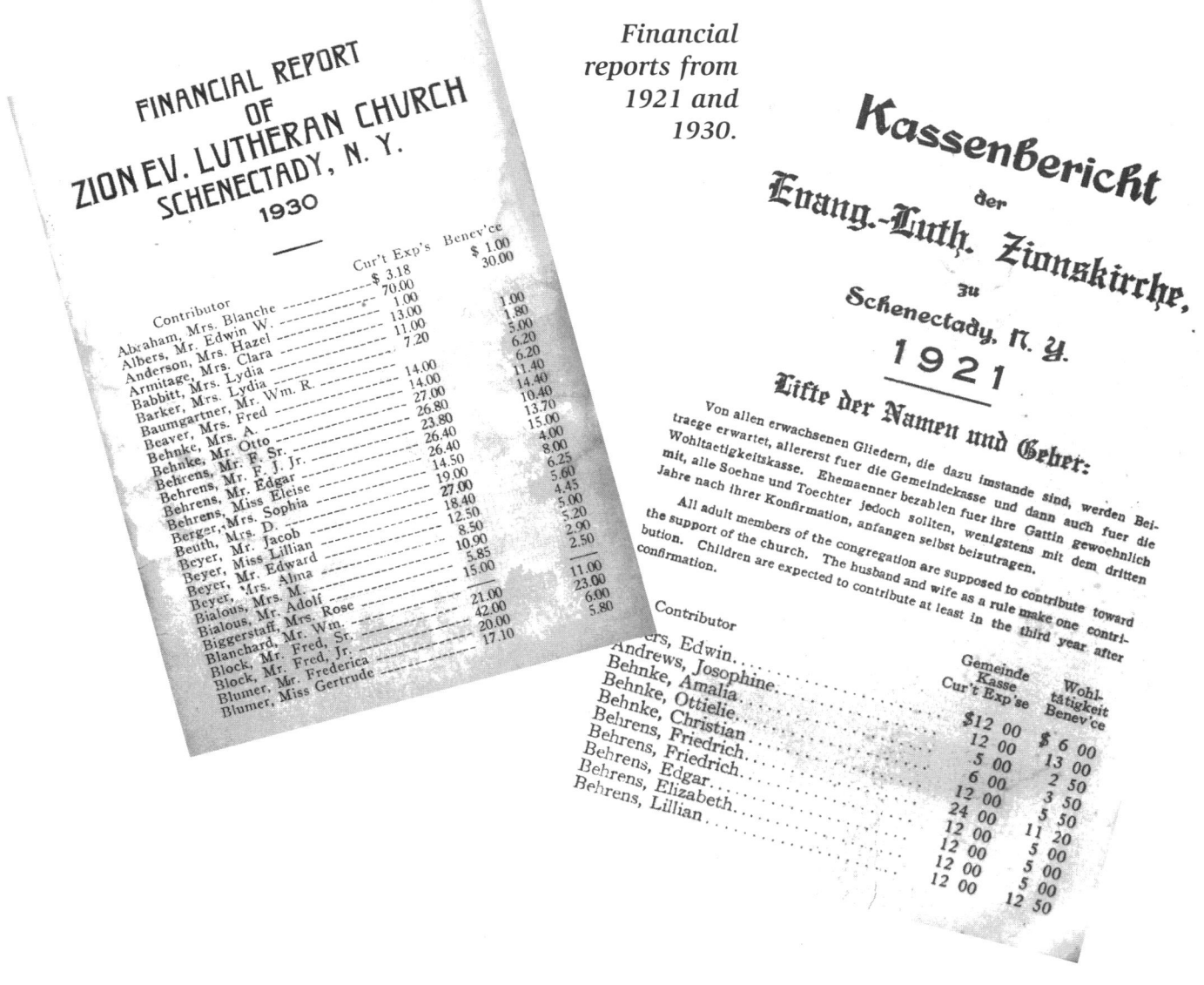

Financial reports from 1921 and 1930.

*The church sanctuary following the redecoration and renovations of 1933.
Note the covering of the two lateral paintings that were shown in photographs on page 21.*

Although the Depression had a dampening effect on Zion and her congregation, it did not cease her building and growth. Many improvements had been made at the church between 1925 and 1930. Some of these included a new boiler system, the construction of the pastor's garage, and the installation of hearing aid equipment. The most notable improvement was the acquisition and installation of a new organ. Building upon a bequest made in 1927, it was resolved on January 29, 1928 to purchase a modern organ as a memorial to Pastor Schulze. One year later a contract with the Skinner Organ Company of Boston, Massachusetts was signed. The new organ, costing in excess of $17,000, was dedicated on October 27, 1929 in a service conducted in both English and German. The dedication service was followed by a week of special activities. Another improvement project was undertaken in 1933. This project included repairing the roof and steeple, squaring the chancel, and redecorating the church. The $8,784 which was required for the completion of the renovations was funded, in part, through borrowing from individual church members at four percent interest. The various church clubs and societies subsequently paid the interest.

Above: Zion's **original organ** which was a small two manual Jackson tracker-action organ installed in November, 1893. It was later sold to St. Matthew's Lutheran Church in Hudson, New York
Right: The **Organ Dedication Souvenir Booklet, October 27, 1929;**
Below: The **new Skinner organ.**

*The **Junior Young People's Society**, 1922. Organized by Pastor Busse in 1920 for newly confirmed young people, the group sought to encourage the study of the Bible, furnish opportunities for education, and foster Christian fellowship. In 1922 the officers included: Gustave Pirk, President; Nellie Dargan, Vice-President; Cornelius Meyer, Secretary; and Albert Buetow, Treasurer.*

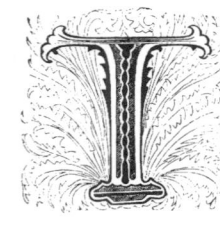

The financial support provided by the social organizations within Zion for the 1933 renovations was not a unique occurrence. By 1930 the members of the congregation could participate in at least six societies and social clubs. The Ladies Aid Society, founded in 1872, the Senior Walther League, organized in 1881, the Zion Lutheran Benefit Society, founded in 1883 for the purpose of providing support during illness or the death of a loved one, and the Zion Sewing Circle, begun in 1893 with 13 original members, were the older organizations. In addition to promoting Christian fellowship in a social setting, the groups provided financial backing and volunteer service for many church projects. The Men's Social Club was the first new group organized during Pastor Busse's tenure. One year later, in 1920, the Junior Walther League was formed for those young people who had completed confirmation. The Ladies Mission Society began in 1927, and lastly in April 20, 1938, the Altar Guild was established to care for the adornments and paraments of the altar.

The formation of the Altar Guild was motivated not only by congregational interest, but also by need. Pastor Busse's wife had provided all the labor required for the care of the communion linens and altar vestments, as well as the maintenance of the sanctuary since her arrival in 1919. However, as the congregation grew and Mrs. Busse's health declined, the work load became unmanageable. After several months of discussion

A 1939 Newpaper article featuring *Zion's Altar Guild*.

The Altar Guild of Zion Lutheran Church held its first anniversary dinner at Sirker's Farm Wednesday night. Members in the picture are: Top, left to right, Miss Elizabeth Burmester, Mrs. William Looman and Mrs. Duane St. Priest. Top Circle, Miss Nellie Peper, Mrs. Florence Pieper and Miss Esther Heck. Lower left circle, Mrs. Charles Bottomley, Mrs. O. C. Busse and Miss Lydia Kling. Right circle, Miss Lillian Beyer, Miss Clara Burmester and Miss Christine Heck.

and planning, the Altar Guild was formed in 1938. Pastor Busse taught the women of the guild the meaning of the colors of the paraments and altar vestments. In addition, he instructed them as to the appropriate, reverent care and preparation of the sacred vessels of the Holy Sacrament. Members of the Altar Guild have continued to faithfully pass this knowledge on to new members for nearly sixty years.

Above: **Men's Social Club, 1922**. Desiring to foster Christian fellowship and increase publicity for the Lutheran Church, Pastor Busse founded the Men's Social Club in 1919. Open to men twenty-one and up, the organization provided many services for property improvements. Some such improvements included the installation of electric lights in the school building, placement of a publicity rack in the church, decoration of the exterior of the church at Christmas time, and a Golden Jubilee gift of a bulletin board to the church. The organization also provided substantial financial contributions throughout the years. In 1922 there were 60 members. Officers included: Ed Burmester, President; H. Lantz, Vice-President; H. Demgen, Secretary; and Theodore Buschmann, Treasurer.

Below: **The Ladies Aid Society, 1922**

Pastor Otto C. Busse   1919-1945

Ladies Aid Society, 1925.

Zion Lutheran Church Men's Social Club Celebrates Its 15th Anniversary

Rev. Otto C. Busse, was the principal speaker at the dinner, pictured above, of the Men's Social Club of Zion Lutheran Church, in celebration of the 15th anniversary of its organization. Duane St. Priest, secretary, served as toastmaster.

Rev. Busse spoke on "Accomplishment and Aspiration", emphasizing the services already performed by the club and spurring it on to greater achievements in the future. A feature of the dinner was group singing led by Emil Wilk, church organist.

Past Presidents include William Schopmann, 1919-1921; J. Edward Burmester, 1922-1923; Charles Gerni, 1924; Walter Ossenfort, 1925-1927; Fred Gerling, 1928; William Looman, 1929-1931; Martin Schulenburg, 1932; Carl Brandt, 1933.

The present officers of the club are president, Albert Muchow; vice-president, William Wolff; secretary, Duane W. St. Priest; treasurer, Theodore H. Bushman, sr., who has served in that capacity continuously since the organization of the club.

The banquet was prepared and served by the Ladies' Mission Society of Zion Lutheran Church.

The arrangement committee consisted of Albert Muchow, chairman; Walter Ossenfort, Harry W. Demgen, Frank Streifert, Carl Derwig, jr., Fred Block, jr., Emil Wilk, Rev. Otto Busse and the present officers of the club.

The members of the club appearing in the photograph are, left row, front to rear, Charles Gerni, Henry Lantz, Otto Andress, E. William Bodenstab, Henry Kleine, Fred Block, Jacob Schuler and Ferdinand Schraeder.

Second row, front to rear, Edwin W. Albers, John Lantz, Louis Pomplim, Paul Pomplin, August Weber, Charles Fasake, Emil Wilk, Fred Looman and John Petersen.

Third row, front to rear, Clarence Law, Fred Holzhauer, Leo Babbitt, Frank Streifert, Adam Fischer, Walter Lathrop, Herman Zamjohl and Willy Peper.

Fourth row, front to rear, Albert Muchow, Herman Bustow, John Koch, Reinhold Zamjohn, Carl Derwig, Louis Meentemeier, Walter Ossenfort, Harry W. Demgen, Herman Maier and William Looman.

Rear row, left to right, Willie Schopmann, Rev. Otto Busse, Duane St. Priest, Theodore H. Bushman and William Wolff.

Cast of the Young People's Play, 1926. <u>Back Row</u> (left to right): Alfred Heck, Oscar Nitchman, Carl Doring, William Horstmyer, Albert Streiffert, and Otto Herderich. <u>Front Row</u> (left to right): Ethel Gerni, Clara Buhrmester, Frederick Ossenfort, Emma Brown, and Rose Platt.

Zion's congregation flourished under Pastor Busse's guidance. In slightly over twenty years, from 1919 to the early 1940's, membership increased by one-half, from approximately 400 confirmed members to 600 members by the beginning of World War II. Many others who were not members also attended Zion on a regular basis. Even more notable than the fifty percent increase in membership was the 200 percent increase in contributions.

During Pastor Busse's pastorate at Zion, he served in several synodical posts as well. He was a visitor of the

Above: ***Zion's ushers, 1930.***

Albany Circuit and president of the Albany Pastoral Conference. He served as a member of the Board of Directors of the Atlantic District of the Evangelical Lutheran Synod of Missouri for several years, and was the first stewardship secretary of the Atlantic District, Lutheran Church - Missouri Synod. In addition to his synod work, he was a chaplain reserve of the 398th Infantry and president of the Schenectady Chapter - Organized Reserve Officers.

Even though the late 1930's and early 1940's brought a renewed prosperity to Zion, the accompanying peace was short-lived. The outbreak of World War II resulted in the United States National Guard being called into service. Recognizing that there would be a great need for ministry to Lutherans in the Armed Services, Pastor Busse requested, and was granted, a leave of absence in January, 1941. Entering with the rank of Major, he resumed his duties as chaplain in the United States Armed Forces.

Left: **Zion's basketball team**, 1940. Back Row (left to right): Coach Al Macholz, Bill Pieper, Bob Weber, Ed Sprenger, Harold Shear. Front Row: Harrison Demgen, Jack Lantz, Bill Weber, Bob Saxby.

Below: **Young men of Zion**, circa 1931. Back row (left to right): Fred Behrens, Bill Looman, (?), Myron Fischer, (?), Fred Block, Bill Mielke, Edgar Behrens. Front row (left to right): Fred Ossenfort, Al Block, Al Buetow, Leo Harke, Al Streifert, Carl Doring.

Opposite page left: **Men's club officers**, circa 1930, "Pinochle players all!" Back row (left to right): Reinhold Zamjohn, Carl Derwig, Mr. Sommemeyer (?). Front row (left to right): Walter Ossenfort, Harry Demgen.

A Ministry By Grace

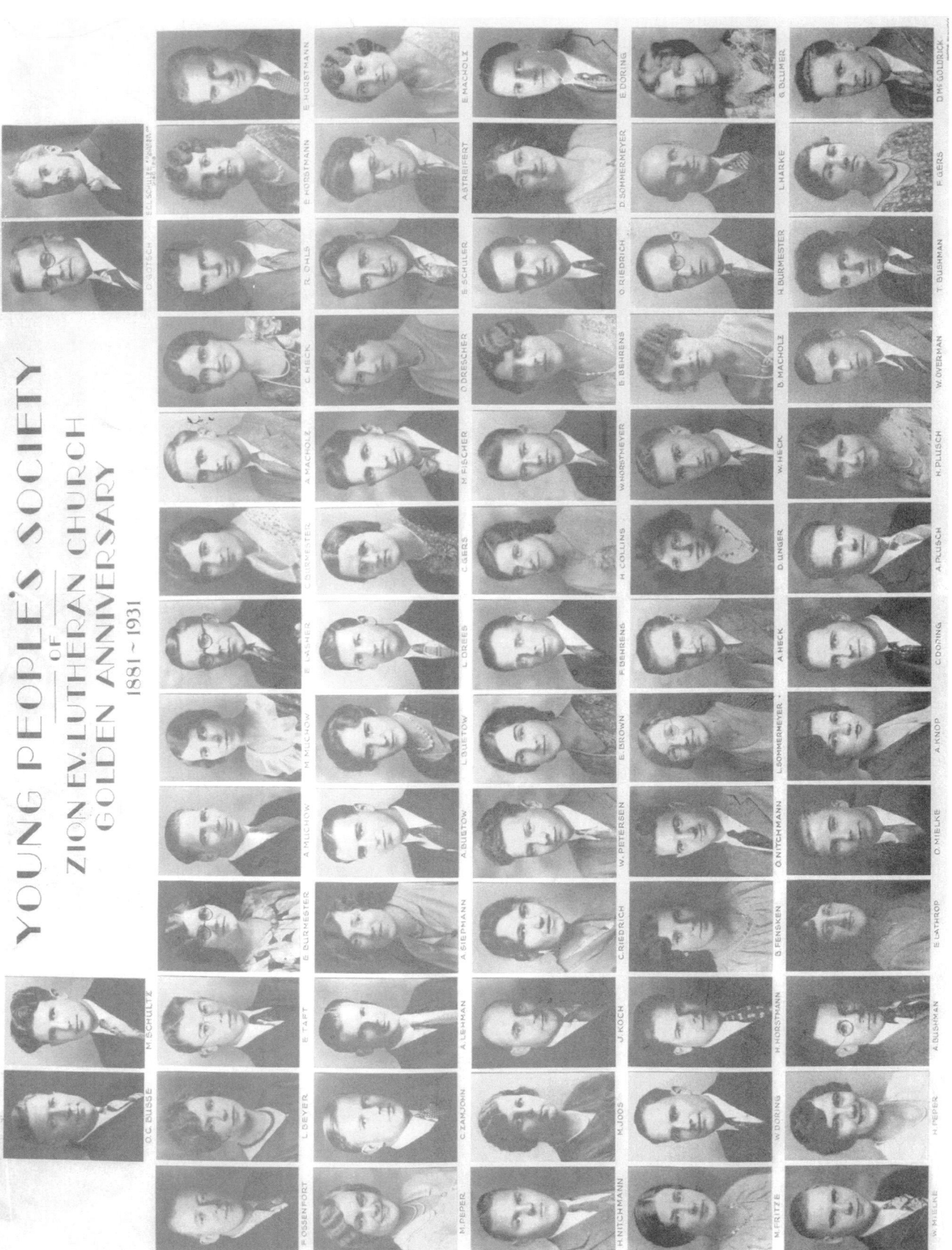

Zion's Young People's Society, 1881-1931. <u>Top Row</u> (left to right): O.C. Busse, M. Schulz, O.Gotsch, E.C.L. Schulze, "Founder of Society, died 1918". <u>Second Row</u>: F. Ossenfort, L.Beyer, E. Taft, E. Burmester, A. Muchow, M. Muchow, E. Lasher, C. Burmester, A. Macholz, C. Heck, R. Ohls, E. Horstmann, E. Horstmann. <u>Third Row</u>: M. Peper, C. Zamjohn, A. Lehman, A. Siepmann, A. Buetow, L. Buetow, L. Drees, C. Gers, M. Fischer, O. Drescher, E. Schuler, A. Streifert, E. Macholz. <u>Fourth Row</u>: H. Nitchmann, M. Joos, J. Koch, C. Riedrich, W. Petersen, E. Brown, F. Behrens, H. Collins, W. Horstmeyer, E. Behrens, O. Riedrich, D. Sommermeyer, E. Doring. <u>Fifth Row</u>: M. Fritze, W. Doring, H. Horstmann, B. Fensken, O. Nitchmann, L. Sommermeyer, A. Heck, D. Unger, W. Heck, B. Macholz, H. Burmester, L. Harke, G. Blumer. <u>Sixth Row</u>: W. Mielke, H. Peper, A. Bushman, E. Lathrop, O. Mielke, A. Knop, C. Doring, A. Plusch, H. Plusch, W. Overman, T. Bushman, F. Gers, D. McGoldrick. Photograph courtesy of Ed Schuler.

During the course of the war, seventy-five other members of Zion were to serve in the military as well. Pastor John Sohn served as interim pastor from March, 1941 until April, 1943. Zion then called Pastor Robert C. Albohm in 1943.

Pastor Busse was first stationed at Camp Lee, Virginia where he served as camp chaplain. It was there that his wife of thirty-seven years passed away in May, 1941. He was later placed in charge of the chaplaincy at Port Terminal, New York, the point of embarkation for the men and women going overseas. In December, 1945 Pastor Busse requested to be relieved as pastor of Zion. His request was granted. In Spring of 1946 he received an Honorable Discharge from active service, having attained the rank of Lieutenant Colonel. After delivering a farewell sermon at Zion, he returned to his native Indiana to become the pastor of St. Paul's Evangelical Lutheran Church in Preble. He served that congregation until his retirement in 1958, and subsequently held the post of Pastor Emeritus of that church. Pastor Busse became an honorary retired chaplain of the United Stated Army in 1950. Throughout the later years of his ministry he served as counselor of the Atlantic and Central Districts of the Synod. He was a member of the Lutheran Service Commission, as well as the Synod's Armed Services Commission, in which he served as secretary. Never forgetting his spiritual family at Zion, he returned to be guest preacher for several of her anniversary services. Pastor Busse passed away on August 21, 1984.

Zion Men's Club Charter Members, Twelve of the 38 members at its 25th Anniversary October 28, 1944. <u>Front Row</u> *(left to right): Carleton Gerni, Theodore H. Bushmann, Pastor Busse, William Schopman, Harry W. Demgen, and Berthold A. Russerow;* <u>Back Row</u> *(left to right): Walter Ossenfort, Martin H. Schulenberg, Walter H. Lathrop, J. Edward Buhrmaster, John Lantz, and Fred Holzhauer. Photograph donated by Harry Demgen, December, 1987.*

Farewell Dinner for Pastor Busse at the Swedish Hall on Albany Street. <u>Front Row</u> *(left to right): (?), Mrs. Bertha Schuler, Pastor Busse, Mrs. Marjorie Albohm, Mrs. Emily Schopman, Mrs. Sophie Bushman;* <u>Back Row</u> *(left to right): Pastor Albohm, Ed Schuler, (?), William Schopman, Theodore Bushman. Photograph donated by Harry Demgen, December, 1987.*

A Ministry By Grace

1919 Confirmation Class
Carl Blumer, Carl Doring, H. Carl Droms, C. Georg Frank, Cornelius Meyer, Oscar Nitschmann, Myron Fischer, Lillian Beyer, Emma Braun, Helena Harke, Erna Heck, Esther Horstmann, Elizabeth Knop, Frieda Siepmann, Nellie Dargan, Dorothea Schopman, Helene Thomae, Helen VerWiebe, Irene VerWiebe

1922 Confirmation Class
Edward Doring, Ernest Droms, Albert Froschauer, William Hahn, Henry Heck, Heinrich Horstmann, William Horstmyer, Robert Koch, Edward Taft, Eleanor Dargan, Nelda Desens, Margaret Fox, Ethel Gerni, Ella Kohl, Hilda Knop, Linna Nitzschmann, Hildegarde Shopmyer, Dorothea Sommermeyer

1923 Confirmation Class
Theo Buschmann, Georg Sengenberger, Walter Horstmann, Edward Lasher, Herbert Dettbarn, Thomas Dargan, Dorothea Unger, Ruth Knop, Hilda Quellhorst, Elsie Horstmann, Mildred Gerni, Esther Meyer, Hazel Buhrmaster, Mildred Nitchmann, Rose Platt, Alice Glindmyer

1924 Confirmation Class
Edward Mordsfeld, Edward Schuler, Clarence Nitchman, George Lohaus, William Pirk, Albert Macholz, Walter Heck, Albert Doring, Frederick Glindmyer, George Droms, Floyd Buhrmaster, Hildegarde VerWiebe, Olga Drescher, Mildred Nyers, Marie Joos, Margaret Kuehn

1925 Confirmation Class
Carl Sengenberger, Albert Streifert, Adalf Platt, Arnold Bushmann, Roy Stigberg, G. Edward Horstmann, Fred Buhrmaster, Howard Froschauer, Edmund Thomae, Otto Mielke, Gertrude Hoeth, Bertha Macholz

1926 Confirmation Class
Carl Glindmyer, Frederick Kramer, Wesley Mordsfeld, Herbert Burmester, George Joos, Hans Willmen, Alphonse Drescher, Arthur Coyner, Frederick Kluth, Stuart Nitchmann, Walter Platt, Herbert Nitzschman, Harry Quellhorst, Herman Kluge, Christine Riedrich, Esther Heck, Mabel Myers, Helen Hartman, Hilda Sengenberger, Lucille Sommermeyer

A Ministry By Grace

1927 Confirmation Class
Walter Joos, Albert Bunkoff, William Kergel, Ernest Heck, William Quellhorst, Marie Fritze, Margaret Corrigan, Ella Doring, Emma Macholz, Mildred Post, Wilhelmina Desens

1928 Confirmation Class
William Blanchard, William Peterson, Fritz Hotopp, George Haupt, John Bowser, Albert Platt, Wilfred Taft, Waldeman Thomae, Helene Haupt, Mildred Knabner, Dorothea Mordsfeld, Dacey Joos, Anita Knop, Dorothy Buhrmaster, Bertha Kergel

1930 Confirmation Class
Walter Schneider, Emil Bialous, Donald Lobb, Carl Shopmyer,
Arnold Willmen, Robert Meyer, Frederick Kluge, Henry Gerling,
Gilbert Gerling, John Knabner, Edward Joos, Esther Platt,
Lillian Schubert, Helene Kramer, Virginia Myers,
Martha Kluth Frieda Doring

A Ministry By Grace

1933 Confirmation Class
John Pierson, Edward Post, Herbert Strelow, Manfred Lueck, Albert Bodenstab, Louis Pomplin, Earl Glindmyer, James Shopmyer, Walter Sengenberger, Clarence Droms, Rudolf Kergel, John Neary, Jane Ledbetter, Marie Heck, Ruth Barker, Elsie Kluth, Helen Kluth, Dorothy Lohmann, Louise Strelow

1939 Confirmation Class
This class was confirmed on Pentacost due to the fact that Pastor Busse had fractured his leg in March.
Robert Brandt, Robert Duerr, Herbert Forst, Richard Snyder, Edgar Peper, John Edward Sprenger, Arthur Johnson, Donald St.Priest, Ruth Lobrecht, Audrey Finch, Margaret Ramlow, Evelyn Weh, Dolores Bowser, Louise Mohlmann, Marion Nichols, Marion Buetow, Ruth Quigg, Marie Oudt, Jane Sprenger

1940 Confirmation Class
James Franklin, Theodore Smith, Harold Shear, Charles Page, John Lantz, Wallace Abraham, Leonard Hollenbeck, Roy Schulenburg, Harrison Demgen, Robert Weber, Richard Sage, Charles Fischer, Frederick Peper, Carl Droms, Norma Pomplin, Shirley Neary, Jean Grobel

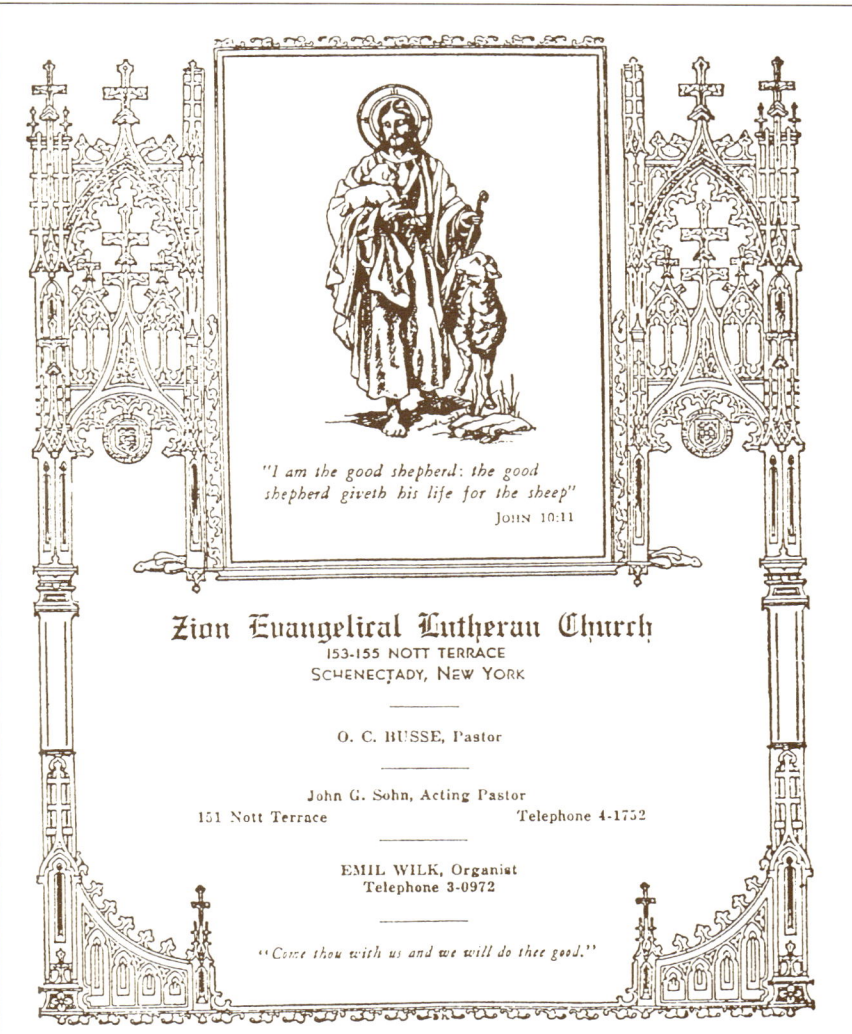

The Transition years

It was during the January 8, 1941 church board meeting that Pastor Busse informed the board that "…the church and the government need his services in the present crisis and that he would be subject to call as chaplain most any time…" The response of the church board was to recommend that a leave of absence be given "during this interim", and requested that Pastor Busse submit names of pastors available at that time. By February 12, 1941, Pastor John Sohn had been appointed acting pastor and presided at the monthly board meeting. The interim arrangements were not without stress however, and during the May 27, 1941 meeting, the church board deemed it appropriate to draft a letter of confidence for Pastor Busse and resolved that the parsonage was to remain closed during his absence. As the one year leave of absence neared its end, Pastor Busse wrote to Zion on January 1, 1942, informing her that his hopes of returning by February 1, 1942 had been "shattered." "…The Government for the time being has seen fit to retain all officers so that the welfare of our beloved country may not suffer…"

Painfully aware of the needs of Zion and of the young servicemen and women facing the distinct possibility of death in war, he requested that Zion make the determination as to whether or not to extend his leave, based solely upon Zion's needs and well-being, and not upon his "personal self." He further stated that "…to insist upon release from the Army now would not only cast a shadow upon my patriotism, but it would also cause the hand of suspicion to rest upon the loyalty of the congregation..." The response of the board was to recommend to the congregation that Pastor Busse's leave be extended one additional year or less if circumstances allowed his return. The stress upon the congregation however continued to grow, and in September, 1942, in a letter to Zion, Pastor Busse again offered to resign due to Zion's "retrogression" since he had been on leave of absence. Once more he expressed his love and concern for Zion and her members. In December, 1942 the board resolved to ask Pastor Sohn to carry on until "a suitable pastor was engaged." In February, 1943 a call was extended to Pastor Robert C. Albohm of Clifton, New Jersey. His acceptance was announced at the March board meeting. At the same meeting Pastor Busse was granted indefinite leave "for the duration." Pastor Albohm was installed on May 2, 1943 at a 4 P.M. service. His father, the Reverend John H. C. Albohm, assisted in the installation ceremony, along with the Reverend H. J. Rippe, president of the Atlantic District, Missouri Synod. Still Zion remained unsettled. Finally, in November, 1945 with the end of World War II at hand, Pastor Busse notified Zion of his impending discharge and for a third time requested that she make a decision as to his pastorate based solely upon her needs. His acceptance of a call in Indiana brought final closure to one of the most difficult periods of Zion's history.[1]

Although the two years following Pastor Busse's departure in January, 1941 were stressful for Zion's congregation, they were not totally devoid of growth and development. On February 12, 1941 it was resolved to recommend to the congregation that the name of Zion be officially changed from "Evangelical Lutheran Zion Church" to "Zion Evangelical Lutheran Church." The name was subsequently changed and the appropriate Articles of Incorporation filed with the City of Schenectady on May 14, 1941. Also during that period the groundwork was laid that would later result in the formation of the Young Married Couples Society. The minutes of the board refer to a resolution on February 11, 1942 requesting that the Ladies Mission and Aid Society and the Men's Club members arrange for a "get-together" for the young married couples of Zion. Still, Zion struggled and yearned for stability.

---

[1] Excerpted from the Official Minutes of Zion's monthly board meetings.

Pastor Robert Carl Albohm (1916-1975) - circa 1943.

The Albohm Era 1943-1975

Stability was found in the person of Pastor Robert Carl Albohm. The son of a Lutheran Church-Missouri Synod pastor, Pastor Albohm was born on September 3, 1916 in Wilkes-Barre, Pennsylvania. He was a graduate of Concordia College in Bronxville, New York, and of Concordia Seminary in St. Louis, Missouri. Prior to his ordination, he served as a missionary-at-large for the Southern District in Florida and also at Trinity Lutheran Church and Grace Lutheran Church of Long Island. He was ordained in July, 1941 and subsequently installed as pastor of Trinity Lutheran Church in Clifton, New Jersey. He came to Zion with his wife of two years, the former Marjorie Rosenast. The first of their three children Judy was born two months later, on June 26. Their son Robert, Jr. was born June 22, 1946, and daughter Marjorie was born on June 5, 1950.

Zion's contribution to the nation's war effort took a variety of forms. The most direct support was through active service in the Armed Forces by fifty of Zion's members. The congregation was blessed that only one member lost his life. Flight Officer David George Koch was killed just as the war was drawing to a close. In April, 1944 a special service was conducted in honor and recognition of the members who were in service to their country. The leadership

Right: Pastor Albohm's call from Zion. Note that the second page (far right) specifies the requirement to preach in English and German.

Diploma of Vocation.

In the name of the Holy Trinity, God the Father, Son, and Holy Ghost. Amen. Having called upon the Lord, our God, for guidance, and in the exercise of the authority with which He has vested His Church on earth, we, the

__Zion__ Evangelical Lutheran Congregation, of __Schenectady, New York__, in lawful meeting assembled on __December 4, 1945__, have decided to call a pastor, who is to preach to us and have the care of our souls. We have elected to this sacred office

the Reverend __Robert C. Albohm__, of __Schenectady N.Y.__

Pursuant to this election, which was held in the fear of God, and with due observance of the order laid down by Him, we herewith extend to our pastor-elect this

SOLEMN CALL.

We ask our pastor-elect, for Jesus' sake, to take charge of the pastoral office in our congregation as speedily as practicable, and to faithfully discharge the same in all its parts, in accordance with the Word of God, and so as to fulfil the detailed conditions hereinafter specified.

We pray God and the Father of our Lord Jesus Christ to convince our pastor-elect by His Holy Spirit that the call which we herewith extend to him is a divine call, to conduct him safely into our midst, and to bless his sacred ministrations among us, to the glory of His name, to the salvation of ourselves and our children, and to the advancement of His glorious kingdom. Amen.

__Zion__ Evangelical Lutheran Congregation of __Schenectady, N.Y.__

Signed this __4th__ day of __December__, A.D. __1945__, in the name of the congregation by the officers.

__Edward E. Weber__ President
__Emil Wilk__ Ass't Secretary

---

of Zion provided additional support for the war effort by making a series of investments in war bonds and actively encouraging individual members of the church to do likewise. A less obvious contribution was made by the congregation by making a number of church rooms available to the City of Schenectady. The rooms were used for a child care center, allowing mothers the freedom to work in the war effort. Later, Zion opened her doors for use as a polling place on Election Day. These efforts of community outreach were to be the beginnings of a trend which continues to this day. Groups such as the Schenectady Rose Society, Mothers of Twins, Girl Scouts, Boy Scouts, Parents Without Partners, and the Carver Community Center have been invited to use Zion's meeting rooms through the years.

> *We authorize and obligate our pastor-elect* to proclaim to us, jointly and severally, the Word of God in its full truth and purity as contained in the canonical writings of the Old and the New Testament and professed in the confessional writings of the Lutheran Church;
>
> to administer the Holy Sacraments in accordance with their divine institution;
>
> to discharge toward all the members of our congregation the functions of a pastor and curate of their souls in an evangelical manner, in particular, to visit the sick and the dying and to admonish indifferent and erring members;
>
> to faithfully guard the spiritual welfare of the younger members of the congregation, in particular, to instruct our catechumens in the Word of God, as it is taught in the Small Catechism of Doctor Martin Luther, and thus prepare them for their first communion;
>
> to guide us in applying the divinely ordained discipline of the church, agreeably to the Word of God;
>
> to serve the congregation as an example by his Christian conduct, and by the grace of God to do all that is possible for him to do, within the limits of his calling, for the upbuilding of our congregation and for the general advancement of the kingdom of Christ.
>
> *to preach in English and in German*
>
> *On the other hand, we obligate ourselves* to receive our pastor-elect as a minister of Jesus Christ, to accord him the honor, love, and obedience which we owe him as such according to the Word of God, and to support his ministrations among us with our diligent and faithful prayers;
>
> to render the discharge of his duties easy for him by cordial one-mindedness and willing readiness, by our peaceable conduct, and in every other way possible;
>
> to provide for his decent maintenance according to our ability, and to that end pay him promptly and regularly a *yearly* salary of $ *2500.00* *and provide a parsonage, the heat to be furnished by the Congregation.* *Edward E Weber President* *Emil Wilk Ass't Secretary*

Against the backdrop of fear and wartime stress, Schenectady flourished. Defense contracts awarded to the General Electric Company and the American Locomotive Company were not only raising the number of employed individuals to unprecedented levels, but raising salaries as well. Zion's membership also grew, and in 1944, with war still raging, the congregation once more began to make plans for expansion. According to the objectives outlined by the Building Committee and approved by the congregation, money would be raised in two consecutive five-year programs. The initial phase in 1945 involved the acquisition of the adjacent property north of the parsonage for $5,750. In 1946 a small piece of land was purchased for the surveyor's fee of $89.00, allowing the back boundary of the property to run in a straight line. The year 1948 saw the completion of the redecoration project which was comprised of the updating of the church interior, office, and meeting rooms. Also in 1948, a new parsonage on Wright Avenue was purchased. The

A Ministry By Grace

Interior of Zion, 1948: Photograph was taken following the redecorations completed in that year. Note the wall treatment replicating a stone structure.

old parsonage was used as the interim location for the nursery and primary Sunday School classes until a new Sunday School wing could be constructed.

The mid-to-late 1940's also saw a growth in the activities and organizations targeting young people and young adults. Cofounded by Pastor and Mrs. Albohm three years after the initial resolution was proposed by Zion's board, the Young Married Couples Society was organized in 1945. Due to the extensive hiring of young employees, especially by General Electric, there were many Lutheran couples who would be in the area for only a short time. The Young Married Couples Society provided a place where they could meet in Christian fellowship to discuss topics of mutual interest and pool their talents. The organization was instrumental in the staffing, supervision, and decoration of the nursery, assisting with family night activities, and making home visitations to Zion's members. Each year the group held a smorgasbord supper and trimmed the church Christmas trees. A typical evening program included dinner (often pot luck), devotions, a business meeting, a religious program such as Bible discussions or mission films, and a social hour. In just two years the society consisted of forty members.

In 1946 the Boys' Club was organized to meet weekly. Within a short time there were thirty-five members, ranging in age from nine to fifteen years old. The club provided a program of athletics and industrial arts, along with Christian fellowship.

In the midst of the postwar growth and development, Zion was blessed with the opportunity to celebrate her 75th Anniversary. To commemorate the event, German services were conducted during the week of October 5, 1947 as a reminder of her heritage. In addition, Pastor Busse returned as an honored guest from Decatur, Indiana for a weeknight service and reception.

Pastor Robert C. Albohm 1943-1975

Left: 75th Anniversary Tea, October 5, 1947. Pictured (left to right) are Marjorie Albohm, Janet Mielke, Beatrice Fischer, Lena Glindmyer, and Louise Grothe. Mrs. Albohm was very involved in Zion's Ladies Aid Society and the Women's Guild, and eventually became the organization's president. She was also active in community affairs and contributed many hours of volunteer service at Ellis Hospital.

The 75th Anniversary Year Church Council, 1947. Front row (left to right): Harrison Demgen, Charles Grothe, Pastor Albohm, Edward Weber, and Charles Fischer. Back row (left to right): Fred Behrens, Otto Mielke, William Mielke, Leo Babbit, J. Edward Sprenger, Sr., Edward Schuler, Henry Streifert, and Emil Wilk.

Christmas, 1960. The two twenty-foot trees were decorated with icicles and lights. In later years the tree ornaments consisted of Chrismons and white lights. Lighted candles were placed on standards in the middle of every tenth pew. Family worship was held at 7PM on Christmas Eve for the Junior High School department. At 11PM the Christmas Eve Service was conducted. The celebration culminated in the Feast of the Nativity of Our Lord on Christmas Day.

A Ministry By Grace

Top left: **"Down on the Farm"** with the Young Married Couples, circa 1951. Skit members included William Kelly, Betty Mead, Peggy Lantz, Rose Borcherding, Connie Young, Vernon Bluhm, Marge Bretney, Jack Lantz, Gene VonFange, Joe Rynasiewicz, George Sauer, and Bob Buescher. Taking part in the square dances were Lois and Charles Fehlau, Glenyce and Randolph Sween, Wilma and Harlan Ecktenkamp, Marzetta Schacher, and Bert Ruediger. George Schacher was the caller, and Martha Sauer directed the production. Photograph courtesy of Connie Young.

Top right: **Mr. Emil W. Wilk.** Zion was served by Mr. Wilk as her organist, choir director, and school teacher from 1899 to 1906. Following a lengthy absence, he returned to Zion in 1930 to assume his prior duties. In addition, he served as the church secretary and taught confirmation classes until 1948. Born on October 1, 1879 in Sheboygan, he died on April 15, 1952. Photograph circa 1947.

Bottom right: Highlights of **the Married Couples** social year included the Society Anniversary Banquet, the Progressive Dinner, and the Steak Roast. Shown in this photograph from the **Second Anniversary Dinner** in 1946 are: front (left to right) Lois Knabner, Connie Young, Eleanor Pintavalle, Pastor Albohm, Marge Read, and Erika Keller. Back: Dr. Edward Pintavalle, John Knabner, Glen Young, Everett Read, and Bill Keller. Photograph courtesy of Connie Young.

Pastor Robert C. Albohm 1943-1975

Above: Zion's **Adult Choir, late 1940's**. Seated with Pastor Albohm are Martha Sprenger Sauer, the choir's director, and Frederick Sauer, Zion's organist.

Below: **Reformation Sunday** services commemorating the posting of Luther's 95 Theses on the door of the castle church in Wittenburg, Germany on October 31, 1517 were the highlight of the fall. This service at Zion in 1952 featured Dr. Oswald Hoffman as guest preacher. Shown in the recessional are: Pastors Arthur Strinke, Albany; Daniel Fiehler, Schenectady - Trinity; Arthur Gerhardt, Albany; Clarence Wollslager, Stuyvesant; Edward Merkel, Scotia; Walter Litke, Colonie; Gary Germann, Glens Falls; Adolph Steinke, Schenectady; Ernest Kunsch, Albany; Paul Buchheimer, Saratoga; Dr. Oswald Hoffman; and Robert C. Albohm, Zion.

A Ministry By Grace

As Zion grew, so too grew the corresponding levels of responsibilities. In the spring of 1946 the feasibility of a vicarage program was discussed. Although the resolution was passed in late 1946 to obtain a Vicar by July, 1947, Zion did not institute the program until the mid-1950's. Pastor Albohm defined a vicar as a theological student who was continuing his training by gathering practical experience in a parish under the supervision of the pastor. The vicar then returned to seminary for his final year of ministerial training. Ideally, the vicarage experience enhanced the student's growth in Christ. The seminary student normally arrived in Schenectady in early autumn and remained through the following July. The supervising pastor supplemented the seminary training through a carefully guided program of total parish involvement. After serving as vicar for nearly one year, the student often culminated his experience by conducting all of the Sunday services for the month of July.

The first vicar to serve at Zion was Darrel Quigley, who began his assignment in 1955. He later went on to become a missionary in Japan for several years, but drowned on August 8, 1966 while attempting to rescue a student. Vicar Quigley was followed by Louis Launhardt,

Above:
*Groundbreaking for the **Parish Education Building**, May 20, 1956. Standing with Pastor Albohm are Vicar Quigley, Mr. C. Grothe, Carl Shopmyer, Art Bodenstab, Bill Ketz, and George Sauer.*

Below:
*Zion as she appeared **before** the groundbreaking ceremony for the Parish Education Building (Sunday School) in 1956.*

Pastor Robert C. Albohm   *1943-1975*

Above:
Work in progress on the **Sunday School wing**, mid-1956.

Below:
Zion after the completion of the **Sunday School wing**.

who served for the 1956-57 season. He had made a career change from mechanical engineering to the ministry. The vicar for the 1957-58 period was Galen Michael. In 1958 Kenneth Potratz came to serve the congregation. Pastor Ervin Gietz, a Lutheran minister previously ordained in a different synod, also served a brief vicarage during the 1958-59 school year. Like Darrel Quigley, Vicar James Weise, who served for the 1959-60 season, later went to Japan as a missionary. James Juergensen came for the 1960-61 school year, followed by Lowell Kramer in 1961. The vicar who served for the 1962-63 period was Henry Lubben. He later became the pastor for the True Light Lutheran Church in Chinatown, New York City, a church with which Zion shared fellowship. John Groh arrived in the fall of 1963 to serve his one year of training. Vicar Groh would later marry Nancy Asher, a daughter of Zion's congregation. In 1965, he added to Zion's tradition of service in the Armed Forces by being commissioned Chaplain Candidate, Second Lieutenant in the Air Force Reserve. He was the first Concordia seminarian to receive such commission. Mervin Huras came to Zion for the period from 1964 through 1965, followed by Roger Beese. Following a career change from science and engineering to the ministry, Herbert Grieves came to serve Zion for the 1966-67 term. He was succeeded by Randall Grauer who worked from 1967 through 1968. The last vicar to serve Zion in the vicarage program was Philip Dorsey. His period of training spanned the 1968-69 school year.

In addition to the staffing changes which were implemented in the mid-1950's, there were structural changes as well. On May 20, 1956 the $140,000 project for the new education wing began with a ground-breaking ceremony and service. Completed in 1957, the new addition contained classrooms for the Nursery, Beginner I, Beginner Department, and Primary Department. The Junior

A Ministry By Grace

Department, as well as other classes, were conducted in remodeled classrooms at the rear of the narthex. New landscaping connected the lobby and outside entrance of the addition to the side entrance of the main church structure. The completion of the project was celebrated in April, 1957 with a processional from the church to the front of the new wing. The outdoor dedication service which followed was conducted by Pastor Albohm. This addition was a major step forward in Zion's continued commitment to providing Christian education for children. Complementing the new structure were many investments which Zion made in educational materials. Members who attended Sunday School during those years remember the many flannelgraphs, filmstrips, religious slides, and 16mm movies which were used to enhance the children's understanding of the Bible.

<u>Top:</u> **Miss Lillian Beyer's Sunday Nursery School** class in the newly completed education wing, 1957.
<u>Middle:</u> Zion's **Sunday morning nursery** in the new Parish Education wing, 1961.
<u>Left:</u>
The **Sunday School Christmas program**, 1959.
<u>Right hand page:</u>
The **Christmas Pageant** presented by the Sunday School Beginners, Kindergarten, and Primary departments, 1960.

Pastor Robert C. Albohm   1943-1975

As the 1950's drew to a close, activities at Zion were at a feverish pace. A spirit of optimism pervaded both the city of Schenectady and Zion. Families moved in and out of the city as the result of positive career changes, and Zion's congregation reflected the changes. Two of the organizations which were active at that time were the Ladies Mission Society, which was affiliated with the Lutheran Women's Missionary League, and the Ladies Aid Society. The Men's Club was affiliated with the Lutheran Layman's League, while Zion's Young People's Society maintained affiliation with the International Walther League. Other organizations included the Married Couples Society, the Adult Lutheran League, and the Altar Guild. All of these groups met to provide fellowship, community service, and Bible study. Church attendance and participation rose each year. Activities such as the ever-popular annual picnic, held originally at Pickney's Grove and later at Tawasentha Park, served to further strengthen and develop a sense of brotherhood among Zion's members.

A Ministry By Grace

On September 18, 1962 the Ladies Aid and the Ladies Mission Societies merged to form the Women's Guild. Originally, the structure of the new organization consisted of eight circles, based upon the geographic location of the members. Later the number of circles was consolidated to six, then to four. Depending upon the membership, some circles met during the daytime, while others in the evening; some met in the church, and others in members' homes. Circle meetings combined project work and devotions. Each circle would adopt a local agency and be involved in one continuing project. The Women's Guild was the benefactor of organizations such as the Glendale Home and the Children's Center. The entire Guild would meet once a month for a group meeting and fellowship hour.

<u>Above top:</u>
Banquet for **Dr. Walter Maier** by the Albany District Walther Leaguers, September 25, 1948.
<u>Above:</u>
The **Men's Club anniversary** banquet held in the mid-1950's. The guest speaker was Pastor Busse. Photograph contributed by Harry Demgen.
<u>Left:</u>
Adult choir rehearsal in 1960 along with junior and senior high singers.

Pastor Robert C. Albohm 1943-1975

Above top: The last officers of the **Ladies Aid Society, 1962.** (Left to right) Ella Weber, Julia Hanke, Beth Bialous, and Helen Macholz.
Directly Above: The oldest members of the **Ladies Aid Society, 1949.** Photograph courtesy of Bea Fischer.
Right: Members of the **Altar Guild** after completing the Easter display of lilies, **1967.**

The sponsoring of annual Mother-Daughter banquets, organizing church meetings and dinners, and providing financial support for a variety of civic organizations were just a few of the many of activities and contributions provided by the Women's Guild for Zion and the general population of Schenectady.

Social programs were not the only areas of Zion to undergo transitions in the early 1960's. The educational programs also experienced change. It was in 1963 that Zion installed her first Youth Director. Patsy Ann Smith was responsible for Zion's activities for teenagers and the training of adult counselors. She was followed by Arthur P. Klausmeier who was installed as Director of Youth Programs in 1965. In addition to the youth program, his responsibilities were expanded to include the Sunday School program, weekday classes, and adult studies. He held this post through February, 1967. Following Mr. Klausmeier's departure for another position, Thaddeus M. Raushi assumed the responsibilities from January, 1968 through September, 1968.

A Ministry By Grace

This page top left: Senior high youth presenting a Living Nativity in December, 1963.
Top right: **Senior high youth retreat, June 1963.**
Middle right: The younger boys were members of the **YMCA Church School Basketball League.** The **1970-71** team placed first in the younger division. That year's team was coached by Walter Klapper (left) and John Larson (right). Members pictured are (front, left to right) Gerd Wolny, Todd Pettersen, William Swanker, and David Avis. In the back row are Michael Arnst, Chris Klapper, and Eric Ossenfort. Members missing from the photograph are Kurt Sprenger, Eric Fischer, Wayne Wissick, and Glen Pelletier.
Bottom right: **The Boys' Senior Basketball team** played in the Protestant Sunday School Senior League at the YMCA. During the **1970-71** season, members included (right to left) Richard Thron, Dave DeForest, Bill Blanchard, Jason Laing, Dana Weber, Bill Daughtery, John Laing, and Bill Weber. Members of the team not shown were John and Dave Bjerklie. They were coached by John Laing, standing at the far left. That year the team won first place in the double elimination playoff. The cheerleaders were (left to right) Wendy Stone, Kristy Huxhold, Cheryl Huxhold, Diane Ritter, and Marion Laing.

Pastor Robert C. Albohm   1943-1975

Above: A **Senior Walther League** outing in **June, 1961**. The Walther League was very active in the early 1960's. Zion's league was affiliated with the International Walther League organization which had a five-point program of worship, service, education, fellowship, and recreation. Young people were eligible to join the Junior Walther League following confirmation, and later graduated to the Senior Walther League. The group met twice monthly. Community services included such activities as assisting with the congregational picnic, Family Night, staffing the Sunday morning nursery, aiding with the clean-up of Zion's cemetery, and caroling at the Ingersoll Home. Members also provided assistance for individual church members who needed an extra set of hands with such chores as yard work or gardening.

Above: Preparations for **Youth Sunday, May 18, 1969**. Shown are Guitarists Brent Wissick, Jutta Laudorn, and Christine Larson. Standing are Tedi Swanker, Laura Serrand, and David Jones. Directing is Adrian Beltran. Photograph courtesy of the Schenectady Gazette.

Left: **Youth Sunday, May 18, 1969**. Approximately twenty-five young musicians assisted in presenting a folk service.

A Ministry By Grace

Right: **The Children's Choir, 1963.**

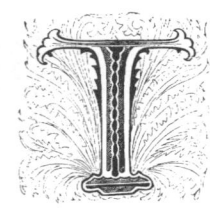The dedication of a staff position to the issues of education and youth underlined Zion's constant concern for the spiritual well-being of her young people. The formation of a Vacation Bible School program was one way which provided for the continuing education of the children during the summer months. The program consisted of three-hour sessions held daily over a two week period. Over 100 students, ranging from nursery school age through junior high level, were taught by nearly thirty-two instructors. Bible study, music, and arts and crafts were combined to provide a fun-filled environment to learn of God's love and to care for one another.

Zion's Weekday School was reestablished in 1965. Meeting either after school or on Saturdays, the Weekday School served several different functions. First and foremost, it was designed to provide a thorough Christian training for youngsters who were at an impressionable age. For the children, the school was an aid in understanding life situations in terms of God's word, while learning through work and play in a Christian environment. It provided the children the opportunity to play and learn with others under the guidance of a trained Christian teacher. The school consisted of Bible study, music, indoor and outdoor play, arts and crafts, and social studies. For the parents, the school was designed to be an aid in the development of the whole child. Its third principal function was that of a mission agency for the congregation, providing community outreach and service. By 1966 there were seventy-five students enrolled.

Pastor Robert C. Albohm   1943-1975

Above: A **parents-teachers meeting in 1971**, reviewing materials to be used in the curriculum.
Right: The October 9, 1966 service celebrating the **twenty-fifth anniversary of Pastor Albohm's ordination**. The Reverend Rudolph Ressmeyer, president of the Atlantic District - Missouri Synod, was the guest preacher. A reception followed.
Below: The **1971 pre-school** learning about Christmas.

A Ministry By Grace

Economic stability and growth continued to bless Schenectady and Zion, and in the mid-1960's the congregation embarked on the most ambitious construction project in Zion's history. Earlier, in 1961, additional land had been acquired north of the church's property next to the Sunday School in the hopes of shielding the church from commercial activities. The houses which stood there were razed and a parking lot installed. In 1962, volunteers remodeled much of the basement area of the church to provide additional space for Sunday School rooms and youth activities. The new construction project would include a two-story addition, the enlargement of the narthex and balcony, and the complete resurfacing of the exterior of the building. With a projected cost of $230,000.00, the program theme was "To the Glory of God and the Beautification of Downtown Schenectady." The entrances facing Nott Terrace were removed and the front wall was lined with windows. A modern entrance through a courtyard featuring a central planting area was constructed facing north, and a second entrance was added on the south side. These new entrances blended Gothic arches with a modern limestone facade. The steeple received new lighting at the base and a cross on the top. The Friendship Room was constructed in front of the Sunday School wing, complete with a kitchenette and much needed storage. The second-story addition provided a multi-purpose room for the music department. Inside, the balcony was enlarged, the altar remodeled and the organ rebuilt. The interior of the church was completely redecorated, retiled, and recarpeted. New pews were installed and the stained glass windows on the north side of the sanctuary were backlighted. The rededication ceremony took place on May 22, 1966. City Manager Peter Roan noted the tremendous improvement

Pastor Robert C. Albohm   *1943-1975*

brought to the neighborhood by the renovation, and stated that it was an example of what could be accomplished with the modernization of downtown buildings. The renovations were completed with a final cost of approximately $268,000.00. The debt which had been incurred was retired in the early 1970's.

Opposite page Top: **The Friendship Room** *during construction.* *Middle:* **The balcony area during construction.** *Bottom:* **Groundbreaking** *for the* **1965 renovations.** *Standing with Pastor Albohm in front of the Parish Education wing are members of the Building Committee. The committee included: Charles Heiden, Bryce Wyman, Edwin Albers, Arthur Bodenstab, Joseph Rynasiewicz, Barry Haber, and Clayton Matney.* *This page Top:* **The balcony** *area* **following completion, 1966.** *Middle:* **The Friendship Room** *following completion,* **1966.** *Bottom:* **Zion's organ and balcony area,** *shown in* **1963.** *The organ consisted of thirty-two ranks and 2,000 pipes. Music has always been very important to Zion, as evidenced by her commitment to the development of a strong music program. Throughout the years from 1945 to 1975 Zion was served by many organists and choir directors. During the mid-1940's, the choirs were directed by Mrs. George Sauer, Jr. The organist from 1949 to 1957 was Dr. Frederick A. White, a musician and nuclear physicist. He returned to the post in 1961, and again from 1967 through 1969. Other organists and directors during that time period included Mrs. Alfred Ford, Mrs. Magdalene York, Mr. Clark Eddy, Ms. Virginia Sands, and Mr. J. Edward Sprenger. Allan Mills then came to Zion to serve as organist and choir director and was in charge of the music education program and the choir school. He also founded the Contate Choir which consisted of a select group of men and boys. It was during his tenure that the position was expanded to Minister of Music. Following Mr. Mills' departure in 1967, organists and choir directors included Adrian Beltran, John Wells, Mrs. Edward Lamby and E. James Cole. When Paul Anderson was appointed both organist and choir director in 1971, there were two children's choirs, a youth choir, and an adult choir, as well as the school of music. During Mr. Anderson's year-long sabbatical in 1972, Zion was served by Richard N. Brinkley and George Moross. Scott Trexler was installed as Minister of Music in 1974.*

A Ministry By Grace

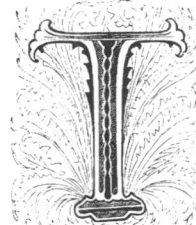

The mid-1960's were not without their sadness, however. Again, the specter of war loomed, as the Viet Nam conflict intensified and drew American involvement. Several of Zion's members were drafted or volunteered for service. Unlike the Korean conflict in the early 1950's in which many had served and none were lost, this time, Zion experienced two losses. Marine Corporal Douglas P. Hallock, son of Mr. and Mrs. James Hallock, was killed in action on April 30, 1967. First Lieutenant Robert Cragin, Jr. of the United States Army, a son of Zion's congregation, lost his life on February 26, 1968. Zion mourned her lost children.

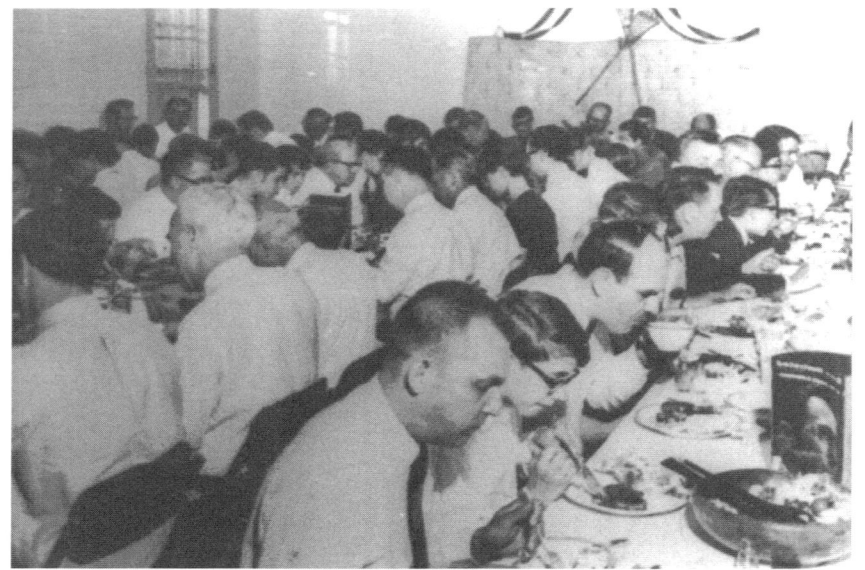

<u>Top:</u> The steeple and bell of Zion underwent several renovations over the years, but even now, the bell is rung manually. As **Werner Boelling, the Sexton in 1971**, can attest, ringing the bell for the morning service was an uplifting experience. <u>Above</u>: **Usher Harry Jones, 1971**. <u>Left</u>: The **Father-Son Banquet of 1970** in the Parish Hall.

Pastor Robert C. Albohm 1943-1975

*Top: **Pastor and Mrs. Aho** and their twin sons, **Brian and Michael**, during their return visit on **March 17, 1974** for an anniversary celebration. Assistant Pastor Aho was a graduate of Concordia College in Bronxville, New York; Concordia Senior College in Fort Wayne, Indiana; and Concordia Seminary in Springfield, Illinois. His work at Zion focused on parish education and youth work. He left Zion in 1971 to accept a call to serve as minister at Our Redeemer Lutheran Church in Riverhead, Long Island. Pastor and Mrs. Aho lost their lives in November, 1976 in a private plane crash when the pilot attempted to land at Suffolk County Airport in heavy fog. Above: **Pastor Bradley** greeting **Harriet and George Halsey** following the service in 1975. Pastor Bradley was a graduate in chemistry from Rutgers University, and received his Master's of Sacred Theology from Princeton Theological Seminary. He then graduated from Concordia Theological Seminary in Springfield, Illinois. Pastor Bradley had received a call to serve as pastor for the University Lutheran Chapel at Ohio State University in Columbus, Ohio. However, following Pastor Albohm's untimely death, he arranged to remain at Zion until the end of 1975.*

As social structures changed in the late 1960's, the decision was made to switch from the vicarage program to the calling of an Assistant Pastor. The staffing was structured so that the Assistant Pastor worked under the supervision of the Senior Pastor. Together they devised new methods and means to more effectively proclaim the gospel in our midst. Assistant Pastor Daniel P. Aho was installed on August 3, 1969. Following his departure to accept another call, Pastor Raymond Sheehan served briefly in early 1972. He was followed by Assistant Pastor L. Richard Bradley, who was installed on June 18, 1972.

Schenectady, by the early 1970's, was beginning to experience the hardships of a city in decline. American Locomotive Company had closed all Schenectady operations in the 1960's, resulting in the loss of employment by a number of Zion's members. The energy crisis which occurred in the early 1970's brought even further unemployment as the General Electric Company began a series of lay-offs. At the same time, downtown Schenectady was watching department stores and specialty shops close, one after another. Zion was considered a "downtown" church, and had prospered as "downtown" had prospered. Schenectady, however, was no longer flourishing as the 1970's were beginning.

A Ministry By Grace

Right:
Many of Zion's members who had moved from Schenectady returned for the congregation's **100th Anniversary celebration**. Two former members, Bill and Carolyn Dutton, were greeted by Pastor Albohm, the Reverend Jacob Preus, and the president of the congregation, Raymond Wojcieszak.

Bottom right: Zion's former pastor and banquet guest of honor, Pastor Otto C. Busse, congratulating Pastor Albohm on the occasion of **Zion's 100th anniversary** at the anniversary banquet held at the Edison Club on November 18, 1972. Also shown are: Elder Gustave Doepke, left, Chairman of the Anniversary Committee; Dr. Oswald C.J. Hoffman, banquet speaker; and Mrs. Norma Finke, Chairman of the Banquet Committee.

Still, the year 1972 was one full of joyous occasions as Zion celebrated her 100th anniversary with a year-long series of events. The centennial celebration in March featured the Reverend Rudolph Ressmeyer as the guest preacher. On May 15, 1972 a special Sunday afternoon service was conducted with the Reverend Jacob A. O. Preus, president of the Lutheran Church-Missouri Synod, featured as guest speaker. There were 715 people in attendance, including members of the congregation, clergy from neighboring churches, and pastors and members of sister Lutheran congregations in the tri-city area. The close relationship between Zion and the city of Schenectady was illustrated by the congratulatory messages received from Mayor Malcolm Ellis and the Schenectady City Manager. A centennial banquet took place on November 18 and featured the Reverend Oswald C. J. Hoffman of the Lutheran Hour radio program as guest speaker. Pastor Otto C. Busse was the guest of honor.

Pastor Robert C. Albohm — 1943-1975

Top: In 1880, Johann and Lisett Knabner's daughter Maria was one of the twenty-six babies baptized by Pastor Schulze. She grew up to marry Jacob Schuler. Born in 1879, she was the **oldest living church member** at the time of Zion's **centennial celebration in 1972**.

Bottom: Easter Sunday attendance is always high, but it actually doubled during the 1950's and 1960's. By 1966, it reached a peak of 1,133 in total attendance for the two morning services. The church was overflowing with worshippers, requiring extra chairs to be placed in whatever space could be found. Volunteers provided valet parking during those years in order to save space in the parking lot. Shown here is the **Easter Service, 1973**.

A Ministry By Grace

1944 Confirmation Class
Audrey Anderson,
Edith Blanchard, Betty Gerling,
Doris Foss, Rita Sadosky,
Doris Zamjohn, Elmer Carter,
Carl Derwig, Allan Drescher,
Joseph Quigg, James Richards,
Harold Sprenger

1945 Confirmation Class
Herbert Hanke, Otto Andress,
Frederick Behrens,
Frank Lathers, William Albers,
Gilbert Priess, Florence Mueller,
Elizabeth Forbes,
Marilyn Babbitt, Olga Sabatelli,
Hildegarde Caster,
Ethel Blanchard,
Marion Snyder,
Arlene Voegtling

1946 Confirmation Class
Kathryn Albers,
John Bodenstab, Ann Buetow,
Walter Herderich,
Lawrence Kahre,
William Lantz,
Rosemary Maute,
Eleanor Mayer, Eleanore,
Matzke, Elmer Priess,
Henry Strathmann

Pastor Robert C. Albohm   *1943-1975*

<u>1947 Confirmation Class</u>
Georgia Baumann, Harry Brand, Frederick Hennig, Gertrude Herderich, Jean Jaquinto, Royle Kressner, Justus Kusserow, John Looman, William Peper, Carl Pieper, Richard Plemenik, Loretta Rogers, Evelyn Sadosky, Carole Sprenger

<u>The Adult Confirmation Class of 1948</u>. Confirmed were: Mrs. Marion Demgen, Joyce Fichtner, Mrs. Constance Wolff, Mrs. Shirley Kuthik, C. Rolland Oswald, Mrs. Rose Lantz, Mrs. Josephine Drescher, Edward Schrom, Paul Wagner, Ewald Wagner, William Wagner, Erna Wagner, Louise Wagner, Hilda Wagner, Margaret Wagner, Irna Wagner, Mrs. Dahlia Cole, Nancylee Finch, Mrs. Martha Spilker, William Wellman, Leonard Harrison, Mrs. Mildred Gerni, Marilyn Havens, Franz Introne, John Borst, and Mrs. Alvina Borst.

<u>1948 Confirmation Class</u>
Joyce Kluth, Betty Dickheuer, Helene Branc, Doris Lobrecht, Elizabeth Alexander, Ann Ketz, Lawrence Trautner, Frederick Anderson, Robert Kahre, Paul Shear, Donald Snyder, William Potter

A Ministry By Grace

Right: 1949 Confirmation Class
Dorothy Carter, Ruth Kusserow, Karoline Peper, Grace Peppas, Marie Schultz, Louise Tants, Eleanor Herderich, Dianne De Lucia, George Wedekind, Roger Hopper

Below: 1950 Confirmation Class
Harry Frendenburg, Otto Tants, Carl Voegtling

1949

1950

Middle right: 1951 Confirmation Class
Edward Andress, Otto Brand, Larence Westerlund, Ronald Arbour, Bertram Schmitz, John Wilson, Robert Alexander, Elizabeth Jamack, Lorraine Wolff

1951

Bottom right: 1952 Confirmation Class
Charles Bialous, Robert Bodenstab, Ulrich Dembowski, Frederick Horstman, Robert Mielke, Frank Sauerbeck, Robert Wallace, Robert Wellwood

1952

Pastor Robert C. Albohm   *1943-1975*

1953 Confirmation Class
Arlene Jenkins, Arleen De Lucia, Gretchen Wedekind, Donna McNab, Rosemarie Caldwell, Marie Behrens, Marlene Ferner, Raymond Cummings, William Katt

1954 Confirmation Class
Else Aschmutat, Manfred Aschmutat, Theodore Bialous, Sue Buhrmaster, Bruce Grams, Elaine Heckeler, Christoper Horstman, Christy Megalaitis, Carolyn Reynolds, Richard Shopmyer, Edward Taft

1955 Confirmation Class
Sandra Shoemaker, Marlene Meier, Carolyn Kellogg, Judith Kellogg, Doris Priess, John Karl, William Priess, Frederick Kluth, Edgar Behrens, Leon Wood, Marie Hoppmann, Karen Oswald

A Ministry By Grace

1956 Confirmation Class
Ellen Banker, George Jamack, Harvey Froschauer, Allan Carpenter, Norma Gayer, Wilhelmina Tants, Shirley Edick, Gracemary Carter, Pamela Hurley, Joel Fischer, Frederick Baumann, David Kugler, Harold Mills, Robert McComb, Robert Strohmaier

1957 Confirmation Class
Judith Albohm, Carolyn Banker, Evelyn Kluth, Dawn Richter, Sandra Rote, Diane Schulenburg, Ralph Beckering, Albert Dettbarn, Glenn Harrison, Alan Horstman, Peter Leuschner, Wilfred Meier, Robert Mills, Richard Plunz, Robert Plunz, David Richter, Gary Rote, Gilbert Strathmann

1958 Confirmation Class
Kerry Edick, Catherine Plunz, Carolyn Forschauer, Irene Tews, Grace Jamack, Marcia McComb, Patricia Grams, Elaine Hanke, Dana Mack, Bruce Oudt, Eugene Kremzier, Albert Pangburn, Thomas Doring, William De Lucia, Delmar Kilmer, Robert Cragin, William Reimann

Pastor Robert C. Albohm   1943-1975

1959 Confirmation Class
Patricia Mowbray, Barbara von Wedel, Doris Strelow, Renate Priess, John Hurley, Peter Fischer, Thomas Kergel, Rocelyn Fernau, Gaile Bodwell, Nancy Bialous, Constance Kilmer, Bonnie Wedekind, Holly Baumann, Carol Seales, Herbert Seales, Annegret Reimer, Maria Bueckner, Margaret Hine

1960 Confirmation Class
Robert Albohm Jr., Jennifer Benham, Barry Bradt, Daniel Bradt, Laura Bradt, Barbara Bushman, Raymond Cipriano, Barbara Finkle, William Hoppmann, Kris Imobersteg, Douglas McCrindle, Alexis Peper, Bruce Pulver, Edward Schuler, Carol Schultz, Edith Selzler, Bonnie Skinner, Dawn Smith

1961 Confirmation Class
Marie Benvit, Elaine Bradshaw, Loren Broc, Marcia Cipriano, Pamela Dutton, Geraldine Francisco, Linda Francisco, Bruce Froschauer, Patricia Furness, Robert Harden, William Harrison, Susan Hinrichs, Mary Karl, Herbert Kressner, Ronald Lommen, Cheryl Pangburn, Robert Pelkey, Janice Queern, Eric Schulenburg, Linda Tews, Bruce Wells

A Ministry By Grace

1962 Confirmation Class
Martha Benham, Barbara Boles, David Bowers, Cynthia Burnley, Cheryl Fischer, Ann Heinkrus, Jeffrey Heinen, James Hine, Charles Hoffman, Janet Kergel, Thomas Kirk, Sharon Matney, Paul Pakan, Dennis Pelkey, David Spooner, Edward VanAernem, Janet Vincent, Louise Wilhelm

1963 Confirmation Class
Nancy Borst, Christiane Buechner, Mark Eiser, Lorna Hoffman, Cheryl Kremzier, Christine Lotey, Francis McKendree, Alan Moodie, William Muller, Deborah O'Brien, Lina Pavia, Marianne Pfitzenmaier, Lynn Pukansky, John Queern, Rosemary Richards, Deborah Sawyer, Neil Schulenburg, Gary Seales, Ellen Spooner, Terry Tews, Nancy Von Nostitz, Ron Wyman

1964 Confirmation Class
Janet Abraham, Marjorie Albohm, Carol Ascher, Karen Burnley, Paula Gravatt, Claudia Heinen, Jacqueline Johnson, Mildred Mills, Elaine Pavia, Kathleen Reilly, Georgianna Richards, Karen Ritter, Sandra Seales, Barbara Wegener, Douglas Barker, James Bazlen, Peter Boles, Howard Cain, Ralph D'Ambrosio, Henry Harden, Gary Jones, Robert Ludke, Glenn MacNeal, Douglas Mead, Terry Ottendorf, Allan Robinson, John Rynasiewicz, Alan Shopmyer, George Van Wagner, Todd Weber, Karl Wegener

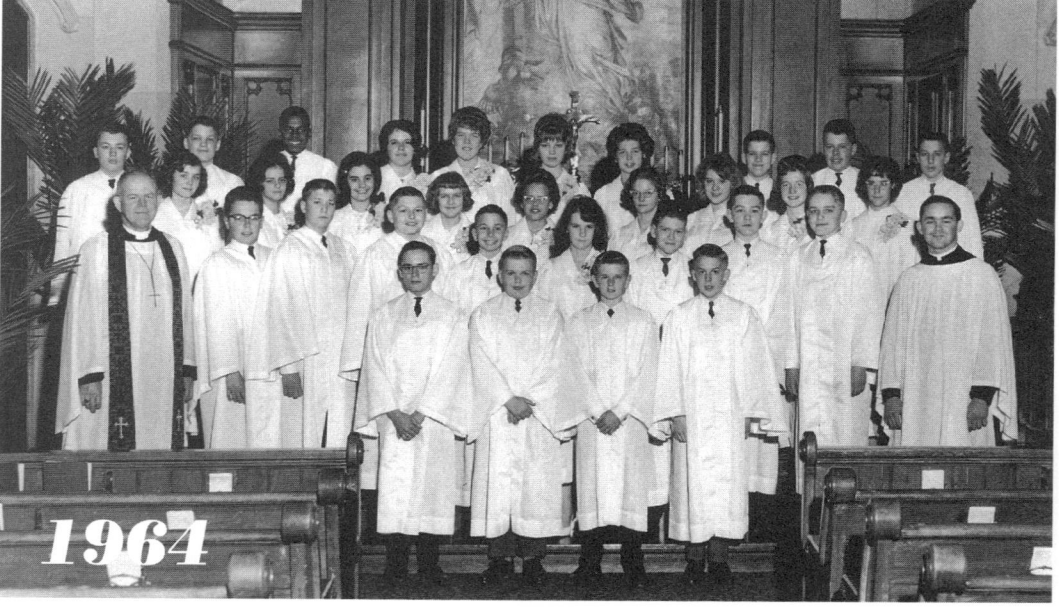

Pastor Robert C. Albohm   1943-1975

1965 Confirmation Class
Richard Bokland, Kirk Borcherding, Carol Bowers, Clayton Bradt, Nancy Commarto, Nikki Campas, David Diederich, Kristy Fischer, Gail Francis, Deborah Friedow, Helen Golden, Dennis Kugler, Charles Lega, Eva Lotey, Robert Naske, Angelika Priess, Edward Schrom, Gail Tews, Dale Wegener, Lee Whitney, Vanessa O'Brien

1966 Confirmation Class
William Bazlen, Sharon Beck, Carol Borst, Wolfgang Bueckner, Diana Cipriano, Joseph D'Ambrosio, Kenneth Dreyfuss, Thomas Finkle, Nancy Gravatt, Deborah Hackebeil, Barbara Herderich, Dale Imobersteg, Richard Lafforthun, Michael Lotey, William Ludke, Douglas Matney, Carrie Moodie, Jill Prazniak, Marolyn Pritchard, Debra Pukansky, Sharon Robinson, Judith Scott, Judy Shopmyer, Karen Smith, Steven Smith, Deborah Swett, Robert Tews, Rodney Weber, Cheryl Zeh

1967 Confirmation Class
Lydia Barker, John Bjerklie, Joan Bradt, James Cornell, Charles D'Ambrosio, Nancy Dick, Jeffrey Eidens, Richard Fahling, Steven Finkle, William Fischer, Donald Gerfin, Lona Giaquinto, Linda Gier, Linda Gunn, David Hertel, Douglas Ives, Jane-Ellen Jerry, James Kerner, David Kuhre, John Laing, Susan Lantz, Carlos Larsen, Monica Lindh, Nadine Martin, Ann Miles, Carol Naske, Donna Ottendorf, Michael Richards, Diane Ritter, Donna Sawyer, Wesley Schrom, Donald Seales, Louise Spuhler, Mark Strand, James Thompson, Kathleen Thron, Richard Thron, Shelley Thyrring, Irving Wallace, Dana Weber

A Ministry By Grace

1968 Confirmation Class

Diane Carlevato, Susan Fahling, Patricia Finkle, Cheryl Huxhold, Ann Kerner, Bethany Klapper, Linda Lathrop, Janet Ludke, Kathleen Lund, Alison McKendree, Cynthia Miles, Cynthia Munk, Linda Ostrander, Lori Prazniak, Linda Richards, Nancy Shopmyer, Catherine Stisser, Patricia Wegener, Andrew Abraham, William Blanchard, David Bushman, David De Forest, Peter Finke, Craig Hauke, Richard Kagel, Clifford Lawrence, Sten Messerschmidt, Richard Schulenburg, Edward Seales, Richard Swett, Robert Swett, Neal Tileschuk, Brent Wissick

1969 Confirmation Class

Lawrence Anderson, Colleen August, Michele Backer, Craig Bakuzonis, Rex Berntson, David Bjerklie, Cathie Borst, Gregory Bradt, Samuel Commarto, John Dreyfuss, Linda Fahling, Lisa Fischer, Susan Galli, William Griset, Cameron Hauke, Karen Huggins, Albert Michael Imobersteg, Alan Kuhre, Barbara Lafforthun, Jason Laing, Debra Lantz, Birgit Laudorn, Rosemarie Lega, William Liermann, Mark McLaud, Gail Pritchard, Susan Pukansky, Lise Raeder, Michael Reilly, Bruce Richards, E. Kenneth Sayers, Marjorie Sayers, Wesley Sayers, Jeffrey Scott, Wayne Spuhler, Wendy Stone, Gordon Thron, Scott Walrath, Mark Weidman, Susan Zeh, Katherine Ziegler

1970 Confirmation Class

Catherine Blohm, Linda Brand, Laura Doell, Julie Falkenberg, Cheryl Grippo, Martha Lathrop, Darlene Leuschner, Cheryl Manderville, Margaret Mills, Sharon Mead, Kimball Moodie, Nancy Oppen, Laura Serrand, Tedi Swanker, Nancy Thron, Michelle Eidens, Steven Borst, Robert Brandt, Michael Eidens, Mark Finke, Ernest Friedow, Randy Giaquinto, James Grippo, David Jones, Peter Kerner, James Matney, Mark Prazniak, Michael Priess, Douglas Sayers, Ralph Schulenburg, Frederick Schultz, David Strand, Michael Thompson, August Weber

Pastor Robert C. Albohm   1943-1975

1971 Confirmation Class
Michael Artist, Peter August, William Brockmann, Dorian DeNegris, Lynn Doell, Eric Fischer, Kurt Gerfin, Christina Harrison, Jeffrey Hanke, Maria Hendrickson, Karl Herderich, Gary Hildreth, Kristy Huxhold, Marian Laing, Paula Liermann, Heather Martin, Deborah Salisbury, Gregory Munk, David Naske, Kurt Ottendorf, Glen Pelletier, Todd Pettersen, Lisa Pintavalle, Peter Predko, Frederick Rifflard, Jean Schultz, Paul Schuman, Kurt Sprenger, Kathleen Vachon, Frederick Wagner, Frederick Winkler

1972 Confirmation Class
Kent Anderson, Davis Avis, Marshall Bradt, Pamela Brady, Thomas Commarto, Robert Edick, Bruce Hanke, Tina Hogan, Christopher Klapper, Raymond Legere, Thomas Lindh, Roger Oudt, James Rickling, Michael Rickling, Mark Rivers, Debra Robinson, Valerie Sayers, Scott Spuhler, James Stone, Thomas Strand, William Swanker, Laura Thron, Sarah Wallace, Edward Walrath, Frederick Wetzel, Wayne Wissick, Gerd Wolny, Steven Zeh

1973 Confirmation Class
Lori August, Karla Berntson, Colleen Bialous, Kirsten Bjerklie, Margaret Blohm, David Borst, Douglas Borst, Robin Burnley, Karen Crandall, Debra Hunsberger, David Huxhold, Jeffrey King, Heidi Lerch, Kathleen McMullen, Paul Mead, Eric Ossenfort, Heidi Ossenfort, Lane Pelletier, Richard Schultz, Millicent Schwenk, Thomas Wagner, Donna Wegener, James Wojcieszak

A Ministry By Grace

1974 Confirmation Class

Linda Aare, Constance Abraham, Marie Andrew, Deborah Artist, Peter Brand, Sharyn Brandt, David Brockmann, Glenn Doell, Kathryn Doepke, Robert Finkle, Luann Fiori, Susan Galusha, Sharon Goldbach, Beth Hendrickson, Walter Herderich, Randall Kramer, Lori Lantz, Wendy Lighthall, Mark Madcharo, Lisa McLaud, James McMullen, Melissa Nehls, Steven Ostrander, Judith Oudt, Paul Pettersen, Robert Pintavalle, Jane Prazniak, Stephanie Predko, Bruce Rivers, Diana Schlensker, Peter Schuman, Lawrence Stone, Dana Swanker, Susan Swett, Paul Tallon, Victoria Vachon, Amy Wallace, Susan Wallace, Karl Weidman, William Winkler, William Young

1975 Confirmation Class

Trudy Adamec, Perry Atkins, Heidi Bergh, Jeannette Blohm, Lynn Bodenstab, Leonard Bradt, William D'Ambrosio, Karla Doepke, Jonathan Finke, Douglas Finkle, Mary Franke, Linda Golden, Beverly Heinen, Margaret Heykes, Donna Hunsberger, Janice King, Lauren Leichman, Linda Leichman, Lia Liermann, Thomas Lighthall, Shelly McLaud, Douglas Mitchell, Kathleen Mitchell, Denise Myers, Eric Raust, Karen Schulenburg, Teri Skeals, Holly Ann VanSchaick, Deborah Wetzel, Catherine Wolff

Pastor Robert C. Albohm 1943-1975

As indicated by the messages of best wishes and congratulations received by Zion throughout the years, her relationship with the city was one of mutual respect and involvement. It then came as no surprise that Zion and her congregation became concerned at the implications which accompanied the proposed zoning changes for many of Schenectady's neighborhoods. One such zoning change would affect the type of business permitted in the Upper Union Street area of Schenectady. Concerned that such a change would allow businesses engaged in vice to enter a residential district, Pastor Albohm felt it necessary to speak out against such a change at the August 19, 1975 City Council meeting. Following his address to the Council he left the podium, only to be stricken by a fatal heart attack. Pastor Albohm was laid to rest in Zion's cemetery near Pastor Schulze.

Once again Zion experienced the premature loss of a beloved pastor. During his thirty-two years of service to God and the members of Zion, Pastor Albohm had established a legacy of ecumenical and civic involvement. Ministering in the Atlantic District for his entire career, he was elected to serve two terms as the vice-president of the Atlantic District of the Lutheran Church-Missouri Synod. He also served as regional vice-president of New York. Pastor Albohm was as a member of the Board of Directors of the Atlantic District and a key contact pastor for the Armed Forces Commission. He served the community as Protestant Chaplain for Schenectady County for five years and was a member of the Human Relations Commission. He was elected president of the Schenectady Rotary Club, and had served on the Board of Directors of a number of local organizations. His influence in community, collegiate, and synodical affairs was widely documented, and his passing was counted as a tremendous loss by all.

Confirmation Class 1918
August Hoffmann, Arthur Bodenstab, Karl Platt, Karl Spilker, Oswald Plunz, Gustav Pisk, Raymond Glindmeyer, H. Wilhelm Braun, Edward Dettbarn, Albert Butow, Luise Schuler, Christine Heck, Maria Lantz, Avada Glindmeyer, Esther Koch, Anna Lohaus, Amalia Thoma, Hilda Dubberke.

The Wildgrube Era
1976-present

Pastor Paul Friedrich Gerhardt Wildgrube - (1935-   ) - circa 1976.

Once more Zion was a congregation in mourning. Although Pastor Bradley had made arrangements to postpone his departure until the end of 1975, the need to call a senior pastor was pressing. As the time for Pastor Bradley's departure drew near, it became clear that Zion was mired in an agonizingly slow process. The prospect of starting the new year without a pastor was a very real possibility, and the congregation searched for an interim solution. The answer was found in Pastor Duane S. Feldmann. At that time Pastor Feldmann was the Lutheran campus pastor at the State University of New York at Albany. He agreed to serve as the guest preacher early in 1976, and proved to be such a popular minister that Zion called him to serve as her associate pastor. Pastor Feldmann was installed in September, 1976.

Meanwhile, the search for a senior pastor continued. That search came to fruition in September, 1976 when Zion called the Reverend Paul Friedrich Gerhardt Wildgrube to serve as her senior pastor. He was installed on November 14, 1976. The son of Helen and the Reverend E.H. Wildgrube, Sr., Pastor Wildgrube was born on September 17, 1935 in New Orleans, Louisiana, where he remained throughout his youth. He received his baccalaureate degree in 1957 and his Master of Divinity degree from Concordia Seminary, St. Louis, Missouri in 1960. He completed additional course work at the University of British Columbia, Vancouver, British Columbia; the Urban Training Center, Chicago, Illinois; the University of Delaware, Newark, Delaware; and the Lutheran Theological Seminary, Philadelphia, Pennsylvania.

Pastor Wildgrube came to Zion with sixteen years of experience gained from serving churches in the Chinese community in Vancouver, British Columbia and in Pennsville, New Jersey. He had also served as Circuit Counselor, New Jersey District of the Lutheran Church-Missouri Synod. Accompanying Pastor Wildgrube was his wife of thirteen years, May Jean (nee Louie) and their three children Michelle, Gregory, and Nathan, ages nine, eight, and six, respectively.

Pastor Duane S. Feldmann served as Zion's Associate Pastor from 1976 to 1982. Born in Wisconsin, he is a graduate of Concordia Senior College in Ft. Wayne, Indiana, and received his Master of Divinity degree from Concordia Seminary-in-Exile, St. Louis, Missouri, in 1974. He served as vicar at St. John's Lutheran Church and the Lutheran Student Center at the University of Arkansas. He then began the Lutheran Campus Ministry at the State University of New York at Albany where he spent two years as the Lutheran Campus Pastor before coming to Zion. Pastor Feldmann accepted a call to serve as a minister in Flushing, New York in January, 1982. He and his wife Susan have two children.

The mid-1970's was a period of unrest for the Lutheran Church-Missouri Synod as well as for Zion. During that time there were political and theological struggles between those who took a moderate stance and those who were conservative. This discord climaxed when the majority of faculty and students of Concordia Seminary walked out and formed the Concordia Seminary in Exile, or Seminex, as it was known. Zion herself struggled with a similar dilemma. In 1978 the Church Council felt that the practices of Zion were more in accord with the American Lutheran Church than those of the Lutheran Church-Missouri Synod. A committee was formed to examine the teachings and practices of The American Lutheran Church, the Association of Lutheran Churches, and the Lutheran Church-Missouri Synod. The final recommendation of the committee was to change affiliation to the American Lutheran Church. The committee also called for a congregational vote on the issue no later than May of 1979. The result of that vote was for Zion to remain a part of the Missouri Synod, even though some of her practices were not in line with those of the Synod. The vote, however, created another dilemma for Zion. Pastor Feldmann was a graduate of Seminex, and as such, his ordination was not recognized by the Missouri Synod. How-ever, Pastor Feldmann decided to avail himself of a conciliatory gesture of the Missouri Synod known as the colloquy program. Following completion of the examination process, the Missouri Synod granted him certification and recognized his ordination. Pastor Feldmann completed the colloquy process in 1980.

Pastor Paul F.G. Wildgrube   *1976-present*

Left: **Zion's staff in the late 1970's** (left to right): Pastors' Secretary, Marie (Pat) Jones; Minister of Music, Scott Trexler; Sexton, Werner Boelling; Pastor Feldmann and Pastor Wildgrube.
Below: **Council Meeting** in the late 1970's.

Left: **Pastor William A. Qualman** served as Assistant Pastor from 1983 to 1987. While he was at Zion, he was the chairman of the Protestant Campus Ministry Council of Union College, chaplain of the Capitol District Single Parents Association, and night chaplain volunteer at Ellis Hospital. Born in New Hampshire and educated in Georgia, Pastor Qualman was a graduate of Concordia Senior College, Ft. Wayne, Indiana. He attended Seminex for one year and graduated from Concordia Theological Seminary in St. Louis, Missouri. Pastor Qualman served a congregation in Greenwood, Mississippi before coming to Zion. After four years with Zion, he accepted a call to serve at Grace Evangelical Lutheran Church in Winter Haven, Florida. He and his wife Lisa have two children, Sarah and Matthew.

A Ministry By Grace

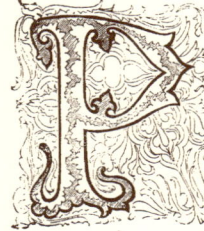

Political and theological struggles notwithstanding, the mid-1970's witnessed the blossoming of Zion's music program. Zion's decision to develop her music program into a strong, integral part of her worship was implemented when Mr. Scott Trexler joined Zion's staff as the Minister of Music in 1974. Mr. Trexler holds a Bachelor of Music degree from Westminster Choir College and a Master of Music degree from the Eastman School of Music. He is a member of the American Guild of Organists and his talent and ability is recognized throughout the northeast. Mr. Trexler has been featured in organ recitals throughout the Capital District, as well as in such renowned places as the Fifth Avenue Presbyterian Church in New York City and the United States Military Academy at West Point. His playing and conducting skills soon developed Zion's program into a model for the Capital District. In 1977, Zion contracted with the M.P. Moeller Company to rebuild the organ. This undertaking included pipe and chest refurbishing, additional pipework, and the construction of a new console. The organ's Trompette rank, dedicated in memory of Pastor Albohm, was installed in 1979. Zion's musical capabilities were further expanded in 1983 with the acquisition of handbells. The initial three octave set of handbells were received as a donation in spring, 1983. The English-style

Pastor Paul F.G. Wildgrube   *1976-present*

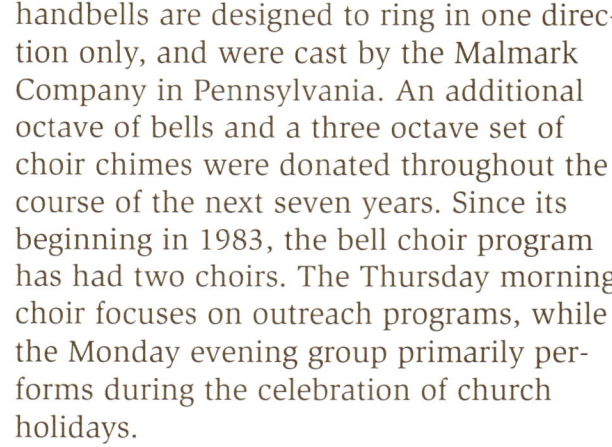

handbells are designed to ring in one direction only, and were cast by the Malmark Company in Pennsylvania. An additional octave of bells and a three octave set of choir chimes were donated throughout the course of the next seven years. Since its beginning in 1983, the bell choir program has had two choirs. The Thursday morning choir focuses on outreach programs, while the Monday evening group primarily performs during the celebration of church holidays.

In addition to the instrumental choirs, Zion's vocal choral groups have grown substantially. Today there are five vocal choirs under Mr. Trexler's supervision. The Primary Choir is for children, grades kindergarten through two, while the Children's Choir features children, grades three through five. The Youth Choir is staffed by young people, grades six through twelve. There are two adult choirs: the Chancel Choir which sings for the 8:30 AM Sunday services; and the Senior Choir, which sings for the 11:00 AM Sunday services and special holiday services. In addition to the normal offerings by Zion's choral groups, the church is frequently the setting for such noted performers as William Whitehead; renowned concert organist, Dr. Paul Manz, of Minneapolis; David Craighead, Professor of Organ at the Eastman School of Music, and the Albany Pro Musica. Andrew Lumsden, of the Lichfield Cathedral in England, presented a concert on the Moeller Organ in 1994.

*Opposite page clockwise: The **Albany Pro Musica** under the direction of David Griggs-Janower, December, **1995**; **Scott Trexler** at the keyboard of the Moeller Organ, 1989; The **Children's Choir** performing with the **Senior Choir**, **1989**; Young men of the **Youth Choir, 1989**. Shown are (left to right): Jeff Specker, Joe Hebert, Aaron Krueger, John Karl, Jr., and Jeremy Kergel. This page top to bottom: **Monday Night Bell Choir** rehearsal. Shown are (left to right): Scott Trexler, Anne Bishop, Mavis Phoenix, Frances Barnes, and Dr. Clara Staunton; **Chancel Choir members, 1996** (left to right): Ann Ardell, Helene Wetzel, Mavis Phoenix, Anne Bishop, Liga Wood, Sara LeCropane, and Karen Wang; The **Thursday Bell Choir** performing at Resurrection Lutheran Church in Latham under the direction of Scott Trexler. Players are (left to right): Connie Young, Ruth Harrison, Jessie Roensch, Florence Johnston, Ella Weber, Mickey Denham, Mary Krueger, and Betty Hancock.*

A Ministry By Grace

With the development of the music program well underway at the time of his arrival, Pastor Wildgrube was able to focus on other aspects of Zion's ministry. Under his leadership, the study of the Bible was significantly expanded. A Thursday morning Bible study group was begun, and Sunday morning classes were broadened. Related courses were designed to acquaint new and prospective members with basic church teachings while providing a review for long-standing congregational members. Courses on Christian living, such as Parent Effectiveness Training have also been offered to support our congregation with practical applications of Biblical teachings. Under Pastor Wildgrube's leadership, the proclamation of the good news of the Gospel, salvation through grace and the love of our Lord, Jesus Christ, continued to be a hallmark of Zion's ministry.

In an effort to extend this message to those members who were unable to attend normal services, Project Compassion was formed in 1976. Its mission was the visitation of Zion's sick and shut-in members by church volunteers. This mission has continued with the Project Care and Concern program spearheaded by Pastor Gordon Johnston. Additionally, the Eucharistic Ministry was developed. This program enabled specially trained lay members of the congregation to bring the sacraments which have been consecrated at the altar to homebound or hospitalized members. In conjunction with Project Compassion and the Eucharistic Ministry, Pastor Wildgrube and the associate pastors regularly call on Zion's homebound members. The ministry to the sick and the elderly has been a significant feature of his tenure at Zion. His care has not only focused on the needs of members who are ill or hospitalized, but of nonmembers as well.

This page top to bottom:
*An **April, 1996 Care Training Session** conducted by Pastor Gordon Johnston. In attendance are Marilyn Martin, Florence Grubey, Helen Franke, Janet Lewis, and Barbara Armstrong; Pastor Wildgrube administering **Home-Bound Communion** to Lydia Kling in the late 1970's; Opposite page top to bottom: Dorothy Hanke with Sunday School children preparing for the **Christmas program, 1975**; Anita Ott leading a combined **Sunday School** class in learning a new song, **1989**; One of the first **Adult Retreats**, held at Camp Hebron in Salem, New York, **1979**.*

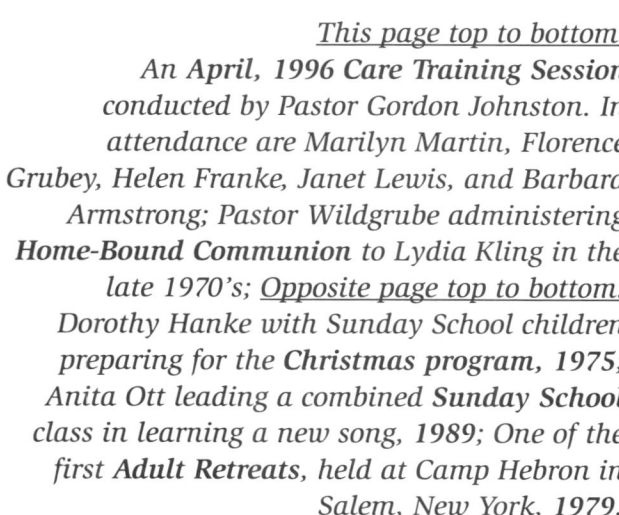

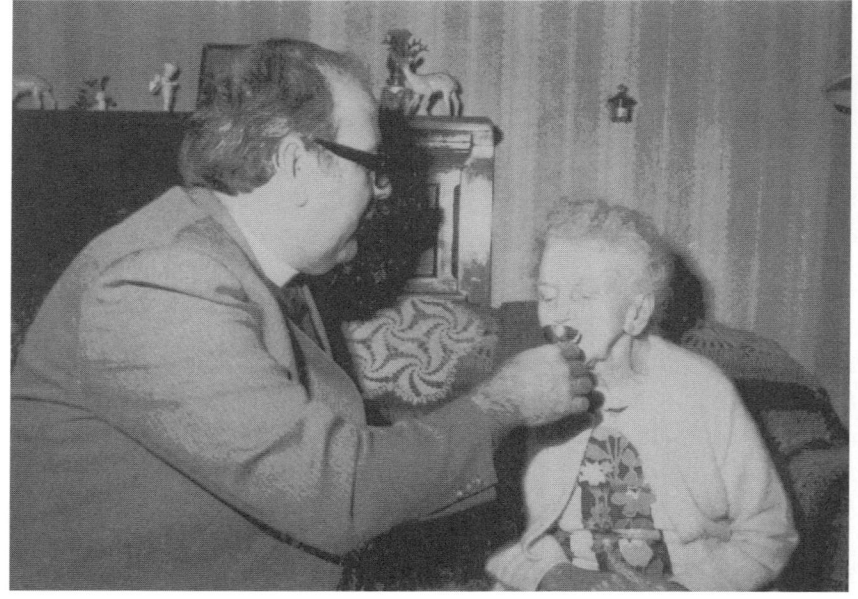

Pastor Paul F.G. Wildgrube *1976-present*

The emphasis on Biblical instruction was not restricted to the adults of the congregation. As in prior years, the education of her children was of utmost importance to Zion's ministry. With the calling of Pastor Wildgrube, Zion had in fact, received a double blessing. His wife Jean was a commissioned deaconess within the Lutheran Church-Missouri Synod. She had been awarded her Bachelor of Arts from Valparaiso University, and served as a Deaconess Intern and subsequently as Deaconess in Vancouver, British Columbia. In 1982 she was asked to serve as Deaconess of Parish Education on a part-time basis, with a concentration on program development for preschool through eighth grade. Although her initial appointment was for only one year, she was requested to continue in that capacity for several more years. During her tenure the educational program flourished. Flannelgraphs and filmstrips gave way to television and videotapes as teaching materials. The Memorization Program of Bible verses was instituted.

A Ministry By Grace

Another initiative implemented under Mrs. Wildgrube's guidance was an award program established to recognize the contributions by Sunday School volunteers and teachers. Honorees have included Jean Wildgrube, Gloria Pettersen, Lynn Doell Manning, Mary Ann Schirmer, Lisa Gallo, Gail Karl, Anita Ott, Karen Coates, Thom Coates, Pat Kergel, Nancy Olsen, Ann Ardell, Edith Calder, Vera Shippey, Ingrid Ekstrom, and Ellen Raust. Always seeking new ways to share the Good News of the Gospel, Mrs. Wildgrube orchestrated the creation of the "Noah's Ark" parade float as a means of witnessing by the children. The ark float was designed and built by Al Finke, and measured 6'x16'x16'. It was entered in Niskayuna's annual Niska-Day Parade and was awarded first place for artistic excellence in floats.

Educational opportunities for children at Zion were never restricted to Sunday mornings. The Weekday School continued to serve as an excellent forum for the development of Christian values and teachings. Bible lessons, music, and crafts

Photographs starting clockwise from this page: Zion's **Nursery School** youngsters learning about the chicks that hatched in their incubator, **April, 1996**; Zion's **Nursery School class, 1989-1990**. Teachers and aides are Ellen Raust, Janice Doepke, Jean Swett, and Jean Wildgrube; A fall, **1982 Weekday School** special activity - biking and a picnic along the Niskayuna Bike Path. With Jean Wildgrube are Celeste Finkle, Chip Gordon, and families; **"Noah's Ark" in the 1986 Niska-Day Parade**; Opening devotions with Superintendent Jean Wildgrube and Pastor Wildgrube at the Weekday School, 1983.

combined to form a curriculum which spanned two quarters of the school year for children grades kindergarten through six. Social activities included swimming, sledding, and pizza parties. A similar program of activities was offered in a week-long Vacation Bible School, with an average attendance exceeding 50 students for the summer sessions. Both programs have continued to this day.

In addition to the Weekday School, Zion's nursery school was established for preschool age children. Developed in response to the changing needs of working families within the church, the Nursery School has proven to be an excellent outreach program. In session five mornings a week, it has provided an opportunity for young children to have lessons in religion, creative art, language development, and literature. The children learn to worship through music, and even participate in a music course conducted by Mr. Trexler. They are provided the unique opportunity to interact with other youngsters in a Christian setting.

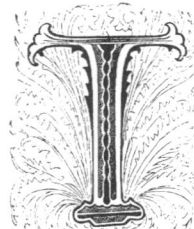

The societal changes which prompted the development of the preschool program affected other facets of Zion as well. One such area was the communion preparation of Zion's young people. Traditionally, celebration of the youths' First Communion coincided with their Confirmation. Confirmation classes extended over a two-year period for young people in grades seven and eight. The Confirmation service was conducted on Palm Sunday. This was subsequently changed to a different Sunday in the Spring. Later, it was determined that unconfirmed children age ten and above were mature enough to receive communion after completing appropriate instruction. That instruction consisted of a twelve-week course of preparation. Confirmation classes continued to be offered at the sixth and seventh grade levels.

Another aspect of change focused upon the role of women within the church. From serving at the altar to reading the Lessons during services; from serving as Eucharistic ministers to serving on the Church Council and as Elders; the involvement of women in all phases of Zion's ministry has grown.

Zion's worship service was also in transition in the late

Above: The **Confirmation class of 1984** on retreat at Camp Son Rise, 1983. *Below left:* The 1983 Confirmation banner - the first of a continuing tradition. *Below right:* The reception for the 1996 Confirmands. Serving cake for the confirmands are Cheryl Adamec and Linda Anker.

Pastor Paul F.G. Wildgrube   1976-present

1970's and early 1980's. The frequency of Holy Communion increased from monthly to bi-weekly during this time period. Beginning in 1982, Holy Communion was celebrated weekly at all services. The option of celebrating processional Communion by use of the Common Cup or the individual cups was also instituted. At the same time, Zion began Saturday evening worship services. In addition, Wednesday evening services were conducted during the summer months for those parishioners who were unable to attend on Sunday mornings.

Above left: **Council members, 1989.** *First row* (left to right): Marilyn Martin, Norma Finke, Joe Masi. *Second row:* Pastor Krueger, Gustave Doepke, Edith Bengtson, Fred Wetzel, Pastor Wildgrube. *Third row:* Jack Bowers, Susan Haswell, Howard Spencer, John Adamec, Jr. *Fourth row:* Tom Ekstrom, Dave McMullan, Thom Coates, Doug Bodenstab. *Fifth row:* Don Berdahl, Phil Schiesswohl, Bob Bowden.
Above right: **Frank Manus and Marilyn Martin welcome Harriet Halsey to worship in 1989.** *Bottom right:* Gloria Pettersen administering the Common Cup during Processional Communion.

A Ministry By Grace

<u>Right:</u> The south side of Zion, with the updated facade and walkway. <u>Below:</u> Pastors Krueger and Wildgrube conducting service at the free-standing altar. Note the T.E. Breitenbach rendition of the Resurrection, 1989.

Changes to Zion's physical structure were predominantly aesthetic during this time period. Classroom I, the large classroom behind the sanctuary used for Adult Bible classes and confirmation classes, was paneled in 1976. In 1980 the south side of the church was updated to match the facade of the front of the church. The planting of shrubs and flowers complemented the remodeled entrance.

By 1980, Zion's altar painting was showing evidence of age and damage, and was cracking and flaking. As this painting of the Resurrection was a favorite with many of the congregation's members, research was done as to the feasibility of restoring the painting. Following consultations with art restoration specialists, it was determined that the best solution was to commission an artist to replicate the original Gogolin painting.

Thomas E. Breitenbach of Altamont, New York was selected to create the reproduction. The new painting was unveiled on November 22, 1981.

At the same time the decision was made to redesign and enlarge the church chancel. The new design provided for a freestanding altar and an enlarged communion rail. This would better accommodate the more frequent celebration of the Blessed Sacrament, while promoting more of a "family" approach to communion. The altar would also be more accessible for the handicapped. Concurrently, the altar decorations were streamlined, which resulted in the altar becoming the focal point of the worship service.

More recently Zion completed a significant remodeling of the church offices. In 1996 a major improvement in the church's computer

Pastor Paul F.G. Wildgrube — 1976-present

Counter clockwise from top left: Buoyed by the experience of commissioning a major piece of **Christian art for the altar,** Zion committed to the formation of a permanent Fine Arts Committee. The principal function of this committee is to make recommendations to the Council on matters of permanent and seasonal decorations within the church building. This mixed media work was the first piece purchased by Zion to be part of her permanent collection. Admiring the work are Fine Art Committee members Bob Mielke, Paul Hansen, Christy Schiesswohl, Pastor Wildgrube and Bonnie Dietrick. Absent are Sandra Bowden and John Adamec, Sr., An **exhibit of crosses, crucifixes and crucifixion** art in the Friendship Room, on loan from the collection of Bob and Sandra Bowden; **The Credence Table** from the original Jay Street Church, on display in the back of the nave. donated by Lydia Kling; Showing their best smiles for the photographer in the **renovated offices in 1996** are Secretary Sue Bowers, Pastors' Secretary Clerinda (Cindy) Grabovsky, and Sexton Doug Ziehm; **Zion's support staff hard at work in 1989** in the office prior to its renovations. On the left is the Pastors' Secretary Elsie Bohne, answering the phone is Sexton Werner Boelling, and at the computer is Assistant Secretary Sue Bowers.

system was installed, complete with upgraded software and a restructured database. The increase in versatility and word and data processing capabilities has allowed Zion to make major improvements in the printed materials which she provides for the congregation. In addition, the Friendship Room was redecorated and refurnished in late 1996. Suitable wallcovering and track lighting were installed to facilitate the exhibition of Christian art.

A Ministry By Grace

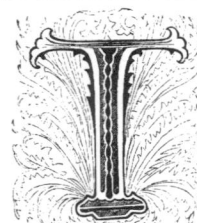

The year 1982 was a year marked with both change and celebration. In February Pastor Feldmann accepted a call to serve a church in Flushing, New York. Pastor Paul Bucheimer of Saratoga Springs and Pastor Gordon Johnston of Schenectady assisted Pastor Wildgrube by making visits to ill and shut-in members, and by teaching confirmation classes. The search committee subsequently extended a call to the Reverend William A. Qualman to serve Zion as her assistant pastor. He accepted and was installed on January 23, 1983.

The highlight of 1982 was the celebration of Zion's 110th anniversary. Activities included a special hymn festival by Dr. Paul Manz, a banquet at the Edison Club, and a special service featuring District President Ronald Fink as the guest preacher. Other functions included a Youth Worship Service, a senior retreat, and a Women's Guild counted cross stitch workshop. There was also an Evangelism Workshop and a program on how to create your own Christmas cards.

As the 1980's progressed, Zion sought to develop a ministry which was more responsive to the needs of the congregation. Society was placing more and more demands on families who were becoming more geographically dispersed. The need for an extension of pastoral care and communication with members led to the initiation of small group ministries known as Shepherding Groups. Pastor Qualman spearheaded the Shepherding Group concept in 1987, until he accepted a call to serve a church in Winter Haven, Florida.

Pastor Wildgrube was assisted with his pastoral duties by Pastor David Grell until Zion called the Reverend Carl A. Krueger to serve as associate pastor. Pastor Krueger was installed on April 17, 1988. In addition to his many ministerial duties, he was charged with the responsibility of expanding the Shepherding program. Under his guidance the program grew to include eight groups that meet regularly for Bible study, prayer, and fellowship. They include the Monday Bible Study, the Guilderland/Voorheesville Group, the Men's Group, the Niskayuna

Pastor Carl A. Krueger served Zion as her associate pastor from 1988 to 1995. Born in Wisconsin, he is a graduate of Concordia Senior College, and of Concordia Seminary, where he was awarded the Master of Divinity degree. He served as vicar at St. John's Lutheran Church, Staten Island, New York. Before coming to Zion, he served parishes in Fulton, New York; Hanover, Massachusetts; and Upper St. Clair, Pennsylvania. During his tenure at Zion, he was appointed Third Vice-President of the Atlantic District of the Lutheran Church-Missouri Synod. After seven years with us, he accepted a call to serve a church in Meridan, Connecticut. He and his wife Nancy have two children, Amy and Aaron.

Pastor Paul F.G. Wildgrube   *1976-present*

Bible Study, the Burnt Hills Group, the Whitney Neighborhood Bible Study, the Mary Circle (the last remaining Women's Guild group), and a Singles Group.

<u>Top to bottom:</u> **Pastor Qualman** addresses the attendants of the dinner held in honor of Pastor Wildgrube's 25th Anniversary in the ministry, 1985. At the head table are (left to right): Lisa Qualman, Pastor Qualman, Millie Fink, Pastor Ron Fink, Pastor Erich Wildgrube, Jean Wildgrube, Pastor Wildgrube, Orna Wildgrube, and Pastor Richard Neuhaus; **Members of the Niskayuna Bible Study, 1996.** Front row (left to right): JoAnn Diamantis, Kim Lorang, Barb Emery, Sue Haswell, and Harriet Halsey. Back row: Liga Wood (Shepherd), Sara LeCropane, Bertha Meyer, Lori Leguire, Diane Bauland, Jean Wildgrube, Ruth Cramer, and Trudy Hudson. Photograph courtesy of Liga Wood; **Members of Zion's Men's Group, 1996.** Enjoying their Saturday morning's repast are (left to right): Glenn Gallo, Tom Cramer, Roger Barnes, Al Dettbarn (Shepherd), Dick Thron, Dave Anker, and Richard Wang. Photograph courtesy of George Halsey; **Members of the Mary Circle at the Advent dinner, 1989.** Seated (left to right) are: Dorothea Schulz, Beth Bialous, Inga Olson, Helene Kramer, Helen Muhlbauer, Katherine Marks, Alma Parker, and Mildred Oudt. The Mary Circle is the last remaining circle of Women's Guild of Zion. Originally chartered in 1962, the Women's Guild was the formed when the Ladies Aid Society and the Ladies Mission Society merged and created a fellowship of women dedicated to prayer, study, and service. Although the Guild underwent many transitions over time, the Mary Circle remains and still pursues its original objectives. The officers for the year of 1996 are: Helene Kramer, Leader; Bettie Hancock, Co-Leader; Ella Weber, Secretary; and Dorothy Henness, Treasurer.

A Ministry By Grace

Another aspect of her ministry which Zion sought to strengthen was that of her educational and youth programs. In an effort to counterbalance the secular demands and influences on the youth of the church, it was decided to expand the professional staff to include a Director of Christian Education and Youth. On October 25, 1987 Deaconess Christine Bauer was called to fill the position. She came to Zion on December 2, 1987.

Both the Senior and Junior High Youth Groups were under the direction of Deaconess Christine, and their activities encompassed service and social functions. The youth had opportunities to participate in youth evangelism visits, caroling to Zion's sick and shut-in members, and visiting senior members in nursing homes. They also enjoyed bike hikes, bowling, progressive dinners, hayrides, roller and ice skating parties and holiday parties. Another major focus of their activities was their attendance at the National Youth Gatherings held every three years in various cities across the nation. Funding for their participation has come from a variety of fund raisers such as car washes, spaghetti dinners, and the sale of Christmas wreaths.

As Director of Christian Education, Deaconess Christine implemented a program which coordinated the entire Sunday School curriculum. In this program, lessons based on the same Bible passage were taught simultaneously to all age groups, but at appropriate levels of sophistication. This unified approach enabled family members to more easily share their lessons with one another.

Pastor Paul F.G. Wildgrube — 1976-present

Left page top: The **Youth Group** sponsored garage sale, May 1995. Proceeds went toward the cost of attending the **1995 National Youth Gathering** in San Antonio, Texas. *Left page bottom:* The youth rolled up their sleeves and pant legs in **May, 1995** when they labored at the **car-wash**. *This page clockwise from top left:* **Deaconess Christine Bauer** is a graduate of Illinois State University and attended Valparaiso University for Theological and Practical Training. She was consecrated into the Diaconate in 1981; Deaconess Christine with the **Youth Group**, in a Sunday morning class; Gloria Pettersen with her Pre-Kindergarten **Sunday School class, 1996**; A **Children's Sermon** with Deaconess Christine during the worship service.

A Ministry By Grace

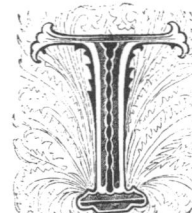

The societal pressures which Zion hoped to combat through the expansion of her professional staff became economic pressures in the early 1990's. The continual downsizing of the General Electric Company had a ripple effect on the entire employment and educational complexion of Schenectady. Again, as in the past, Zion mirrored these changes. In the face of severe budgetary problems and the declining size of the Schenectady community, the Ministry and Staffing Committee was formed to evaluate Zion's staffing needs. It was the difficult recommendation of the committee that the position of Director of Youth and Christian Education be eliminated. At the same time as the committee was working in 1995, Pastor Krueger accepted a call to serve a church in Meridan, Connecticut. Deaconess Bauer subsequently accepted a position in the Midwest, leaving Zion in June, 1996. Pastor Gordon Johnston once more agreed to serve as assisting pastor in 1995. Zion was in the pro-

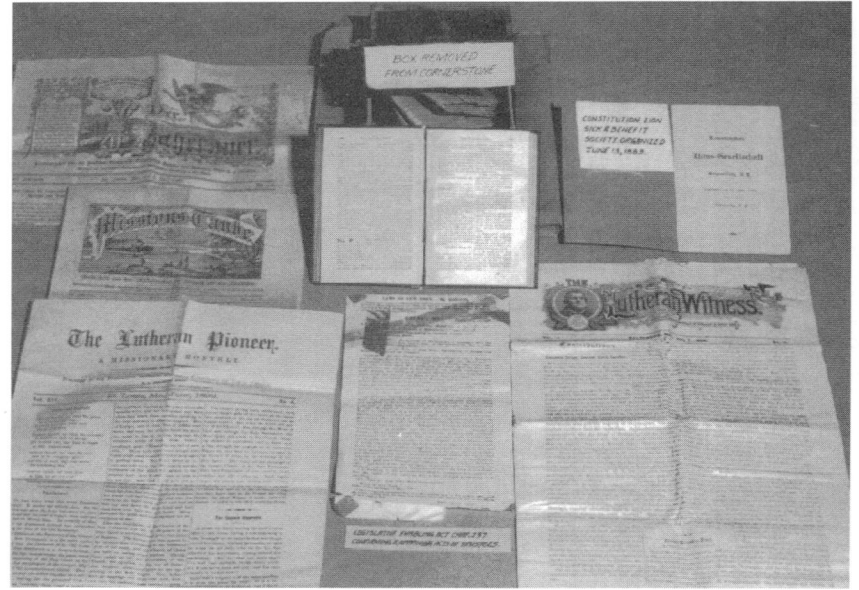

*Top: **Area pastors meeting** with Dr. Oswald Hoffman on **March 17, 1992** in honor of Zion's 120th Anniversary. Middle: Contents of the cornerstone of Zion, opened 1992. Bottom: **Pastor Krueger** and his family at the **Farewell Dinner** in their honor. With the Kruegers is Council President Phil Schiesswohl.*

Pastor Paul F.G. Wildgrube — 1976-present

Right:
Pastor Gordon E. Johnston *was ordained into the pastoral ministry in 1956. His first call was to serve the Lutheran Church of the Resurrection in Latham, New York. He remained there until 1960, when he accepted a call to serve at St. Matthew Lutheran Church in Hastings-on-Hudson, New York. While at St. Matthews, Pastor Johnston began his chaplaincy training. He was commissioned Hospital Chaplain of the Atlantic District in 1969, and subsequently ministered in New York City hospitals from 1969 through 1976. In 1976 he returned to the Schenectady area to accept the position of Coordinator of Pastoral Care at Ellis Hospital. He formally retired in 1992, and is currently serving part-time as the ecumenical chaplain at the Good Samaritan Lutheran Home in Albany and at the Albany Medical Center. Following the departure of Pastor Krueger, Pastor Johnston agreed to serve Zion as an assisting pastor.*

cess of calling an Assistant Pastor at the time of publication of this book.

Weather also played a role in making the winter of 1995-96 a difficult one. Heavy rains coupled with a sudden January thaw resulted in the flooding of the church basement. When Doug Ziehm responded to a concerned call at 6:00 PM from the night manager of the Day's Inn next to the church, he found that over 65,000 gallons of water already covered the basement floors to a depth of eighteen inches. His quick action, along with those of other volunteers who labored through the night minimized the damage. Although the destruction was repaired and the interior of the basement renovated, the damage to the church records has been more difficult and tedious to reverse. Church archivist Bob Mielke has dedicated much time and labor in the preservation and restoration of the water-soaked documents.

Center: Howard Raust and Bob Dietrick removing water-logged flooring from one of the classrooms in the basement, **January, 1996**.
Bottom: Sexton Doug Ziehm and a fellow volunteer cleaning-up the Treasury/Records room, **January, 1996**.

A Ministry By Grace

Even with setbacks such as these, Zion continues to serve God, her congregation, and the community. In recent years, Zion has participated in the Sacred Spaces Tour held annually in Schenectady. Pastor Wildgrube has continued to be very active in the Lutheran Church-Missouri Synod: serving as chairman of the Atlantic District Pastoral Conference, as a member of the Commission of Adjudication of the Atlantic District, and as vice-president of the Atlantic District of the Missouri Synod. He has also been very active in community affairs: serving on the Pastoral Advisory Board of Ellis Hospital, the Medical Ethics Board of St. Clare's Hospital, and the Board of Directors of Hospice of Schenectady. In addition, he served as president of the Samaritan Counseling Center, as vice-president of the Vale Cemetery Association, and on the Board of Directors of Rotary, Schenectady.

Members of Zion's congregation regularly volunteer in community service activities such as Habitat for Humanity, the Schenectady Inner-City Mission (SICM), and the Home Furnishings Program. Within the congregation, the Anniversary Committee has been meeting for over two years, planning the various celebration activities for the upcoming 125th Anniversary of Zion. In all of her works, not only those today, but also those planned for the future, the ministry of Zion remains the same; justified by grace through faith in Jesus Christ. The message of God's love remains Zion's ministry of and by grace.

This page top to bottom: Members of the 125th Anniversary Steering Committee. Seated (left to right) are Roger Barnes, Bob Mielke, Chairman Sue Haswell, Christina Knee, Norma Finke, Jean Wildgrube, Pastor Wildgrube, and Dick Thron. Absent are Steve Rapsard, Marge Albohm Palmer, Kim Lorang, and Dave McMullan; Pete and Lauri Grande rejoice at the baptism of their son Dominic. Aunts Michelle (Skeals) DiPace and Sheila Mulki were Dominic's sponsors.

Pastor Paul F.G. Wildgrube *1976-present*

<u>1976 Confirmation Class</u>
Peter Aare, Martin Anderson, Brent Beltran, Ingrid Bergh, Lisa Brand, Wayne Carlson, Kim DeForge, Paul Dreyfuss, Nancy Galusha, Robert Hanke, William Herderich, Scott Huxhold, Christoper Laing, Cheryl Lantz, Jill McLaud, Rebecca Myers, Susan Ossenfort, David Prazniak, Debra Schultz, Sandra Swett, Steven Ulmer, Katherine Williams, Robert Wojcieszak, Jonathan Wolff, Deborah Zeh

<u>1977 Confirmation Class</u>
Nancy Atkins, Stephan Avis, Alyson Beltran, Timothy Bialous, Diane Bodenstab, Lynn Brandt, Colleen Colleton, Jan D'Ambrosio, Elizabeth Demgen, Brian Kaczmarek, Kevin Kaczmarek, Lynn Kislar, Gary Kressner, Nelson Raust, Nina Raust, Brian Rohan, Michael Rohan, David Ruediger, Frederick Schlensker, Christian Schwenk, Laurie Skeals, Michele Skeals, Ellen Stigberg, Emily Wallace

<u>1978 Confirmation Class</u>
Stephen Andrews, Laurel Atkins, John August, Wendy Bodenstab, Kirk Broecker, Mary Buck, Sharon Carlson, Colleen Hiley, James Kahre, John Koehler, Robert Koehler, Kristine Krueger, Douglas Liermann, Scott Madcharo, Dwayne Munk, Craig Rasmussen, Christopher Schworm, Amy Tileschuk, Sherri Trump

A Ministry By Grace

1979 Confirmation Class
Darci Calder, Darrin Beltran, Sharon Bodenstab, Lynda Brockmann, Derrick DeForge, Denise Dietrick, Kathryn Gerfin, Kristine Hutans, David Johnston, Michael Kaczmarek, Dawn Keegan, William Krein, Jeffrey Kussner, Jennifer Ott, Timothy Pelletier, Christine Pettersen, Ruth Pettersen, Janice Raeder, Amanda Ossenfort, Tanya Rasmussen, Kira Raust, Kimberly Krueger, Cynthia Ray, Cynthia Schwind, Timothy Skeals

1980 Confirmation Class
Paul August, Stephanie Bowers, Melanie Broecker, Denise Coil, Kandy Doepke, Mark Keegan, Jeffrey Lantz, Danyal McLaud, Mark Phoenix, David Wetzel

1981 Confirmation Class
Cheri Bodenstab, Craig Koehler, Elizabeth Buck, Terrance Colleton, Heather DeForge, Kordelia Hutans, Karen Madcharo, Allan Miller, Susan Mitchell, Lisa Renz, Timothy Ramage, Colleen Reynolds, Kimberly Riggert, Ann Trump, Eric Schlensker, Steven Schwind, Karen Shopmyer, Rebecca Wegener, Michelle Wildgrube

Pastor Paul F.G. Wildgrube   *1976-present*

1983 Confirmation Class
Jennifer Andrews,
Kenneth Buhrmaster,
Leslie Comerford,
Bryan Ekstrom, Peter Hansen,
Jonathan Krueger,
Lauren Miller, Susal Ray,
Catherine Rasmussen, Amy
Renz, Deborah Smith,
Ruth Stigberg, Eric Stigberg,
Mary VanAernem,
Gregory Wildgrube

1984 Confirmation Class
Craig Becker, Derek Bodenstab,
James Boyd, Thomas Carreno,
Joe Anne Clark,
Gina D'Alessandris,
Jeffrey DeTeso, Alan Devernoe,
Elizabeth Emery,
Dustin Ferraro, Sherri Kahre,
Sandra Karl, Erik Koch,
John Larson, Mark Liebich,
James Marx, Jason Marx,
Traci McNamara, Anke Richter,
Mark Schobert, Richard
Shopmyer, Raymond
Strohmaier, Stacey Tripp,
Nathan Wildgrube,
Marc Williams, John Winkler

1985 Confirmation Class
Heather Behrens, Peter Borgia,
Wendy Elmendorf,
Rebecca Bowdish,
David Hansen, Robert Oeser,
Gregory Horlbeck,
Kristi Isabella, David O'Grady,
Michael Kaczynski,
Matthew Kergel,
Michael Menzer, Tiffany Sharp,
Samantha Ramage,
Shelley Riggert, Christy Schobert,
Elizabeth Specker,
Stacey VanAernem,
Katherine Winn

A Ministry By Grace

<u>1986 Confirmation Class</u>
Neil Buhrmaster,
Rebecca Emery,
Matthew Engelke, John Haun,
Joseph Hebert, Susan Borst,
Stacey Riggert, Karen Smith,
Laurie Strohmaier,
Kristine Vrtiak

<u>1987 Confirmation Class</u>
Andrew Bishop, Steven Boyd,
Mary Coates, Rachel DeLeso,
David Devernoe, John Karl,
Jason Koch, Chad Propper,
Nicole Richards, Neil Schirmer,
Barbara Smith, Daniel Ziehm

<u>1989 Confirmation Class</u>
Kendahl Baldwin,
Michael Bodenstab,
Derek Devernoe,
Melissa Duncan, Amy Krueger,
Christine Moore,
Joseph Nacco, Brian Shopmyer

Pastor Paul F.G. Wildgrube *1976-present*

1990 Confirmation Class
Natalee Blanchard, Jennifer Malone, Karen Bendt, James Coates, Philip DelPrincipe, Susanna Gordon, Lisa Kaczynski, Steven Lamby, Heather Moore, Leanna O'Grady, Curt Propper, Thomas Richards, Peronelle Schiesswohl, Bryan Tracy, John Wright

1991 Confirmation Class
Eric Anker, Benjamin Emery, Julian Grant, Cory Hagin, Christoper Haun, Aaron Krueger, Amanda Nacco, Elisa O'Grady, Aaron Schulte, George Serrill, Elizabeth Skinner, Naylor Taliaferro

1992 Confirmation Class
Lori Applegate, Jennifer DelPrincipe, Matthew Knodler, Matthew McMullan, Suzanne Shopmyer, Katrina Sokal, Justine Wright, Ainsley Gordon

A Ministry By Grace

1993 Confirmation Class
Peter Ardell, Christopher Bishop, Lynda Chase, Karl Dettbarn, Travis Griffith, Brian Keil, Zachary Kergel, Alan Kratzke, Eric Lamby, Jessica Love, Victoria Mancini, Kimberly Moore, Sara Propper, Amanda Wang

1994 Confirmation Class
Stephen Bendt, Peter Berrian, Christina Chase, Erin Faltin, Tricia Gordon, Matthew Herron, Judith Kergel, Sarah Knodler, Jon Lorang, Abigail Mancini, Michele Priess, Joseph Prusch, Kathryn Schulte

Pastor Paul F.G. Wildgrube   *1976-present*

1995

<u>1995 Confirmation Class</u>
Erik Berrian, Jo-Anne Chase, William Finkle, Jessica Gallo, Scott Heap, Chrystean Keil, Lindsey Maioriello, Gretchen Olander, Alicia Olsen, Caitlin Schiesswohl

<u>1996 Confirmation Class</u>
Meredith Bodenstab, Travis Faltin, Brian Ford, Michael Foster, Caroline Gordon, Elizabeth Isabella, William Kehrig, Steven Priess, Christine Prusch, Danielle Seaman

1996

A Ministry By Grace

Fun and Fellowship...

Top to bottom: Bob Dietrick clowns around at the **Annual Church Picnic** at Blatnick Park, circa 1990; Pastor Wildgrube and Shirley Menzer-Dorstek discuss the finer points of grilling wurst while John Karl, Sr. supplies the labor at the **Annual Church Picnic**; German heritage aside, its time for the Electric Slide, as the congregation celebrates the upcoming **125th Anniversary of Zion** at the Oktoberfest.

Above and left: **Pastor's family join in his 35th Anniversary in the ministry. With Pastor Wildgrube are Drew Lochte, Michelle Wildgrube-Lochte, Jean, and Gregory; Herb Leichman looks on as Zion's Sunday School classes join in congratulating Pastor Wildgrube in the celebration.**

Pastor Paul F.G. Wildgrube   *1976-present*

Helping Hands...

Zion's volunteers donate an extraordinary amount of time each month in order to keep the church functioning smoothly. For example, each week the Altar Guild, the financial secretary and assistants, the ushers, the greeters, the acolytes, the communion assistants, and the readers assist in the Saturday and Sunday worship services. Throughout the year volunteers deliver flowers to the sick, make banners for the Confirmation class, decorate the Christmas tree and coordinate the many receptions. Other volunteers serve on the Church Council, the Stewardship Committee, the Memorial Committee, the Missions Committee, the Parish Education Committee, the Nursery Staff, the Evangelism Committee, the Social Ministry Committee, the Music Committee, the Buildings and Grounds Committee, the Cemetery Committee, and the Fine Arts Committee. The host of workers involved in the Sunday School serve as teachers and support staff. It is through their labors of love that Zion thrives and serves the Lord. <u>Photographs clockwise top to bottom:</u> **Zion's Council, 1996.** Pictured front row (left to right): Roger Barnes, Dave McMullan, Gloria Pettersen, Adrian Beltran, Peter Brand, and Valerie Schonewald. Back row: Sue Stewart, Bill Thompson, Don Blake, Phil Schiesswohl, president, Doug Bodenstab, Dick Thron, Pastor Wildgrube, and Bruce Heap. Absent are: Sue Haswell, Larry Olsen, Beverly Andrews, Jim Seaman, Marilyn Rockefeller, and Bill Young; **Dave Anker ushering, 1996; Dick and Susan Thron** are assisted by their granddaughter, Jessica Vollor, in greeting worshipers, **1996; Altar Guild members** Cindy Schulte and Shirley Menzer-Dorstek fill the individual cups in preparation for communion, 1996.